I0006482

**NIST Special Publication 800-48
Revision 1**

Guide to Securing Legacy IEEE 802.11
Wireless Networks

*Recommendations of the National
Institute of Standards and Technology*

**Karen Scarfone
Derrick Dicoi
Matthew Sexton
Cyrus Tibbs**

C O M P U T E R   S E C U R I T Y

Computer Security Division
Information Technology Laboratory
National Institute of Standards and Technology
Gaithersburg, MD 20899-8930

July 2008

U.S. Department of Commerce

Carlos M. Gutierrez, Secretary

National Institute of Standards and Technology

James M. Turner, Deputy Director

Reports on Computer Systems Technology

The Information Technology Laboratory (ITL) at the National Institute of Standards and Technology (NIST) promotes the U.S. economy and public welfare by providing technical leadership for the nation's measurement and standards infrastructure. ITL develops tests, test methods, reference data, proof of concept implementations, and technical analysis to advance the development and productive use of information technology. ITL's responsibilities include the development of technical, physical, administrative, and management standards and guidelines for the cost-effective security and privacy of sensitive unclassified information in Federal computer systems. This Special Publication 800-series reports on ITL's research, guidance, and outreach efforts in computer security and its collaborative activities with industry, government, and academic organizations.

Certain commercial entities, equipment, or materials may be identified in this document in order to describe an experimental procedure or concept adequately. Such identification is not intended to imply recommendation or endorsement by the National Institute of Standards and Technology, nor is it intended to imply that the entities, materials, or equipment are necessarily the best available for the purpose.

Acknowledgments

The authors, Karen Scarfone of the National Institute of Standards and Technology (NIST) and Derrick Dicoi, Matthew Sexton, and Cyrus Tibbs of Booz Allen Hamilton, wish to thank their colleagues who reviewed drafts of this document and contributed to its technical content. The authors would like to acknowledge Sheila Frankel, Tim Grance, Tom Karygiannis, and Terry D. Hahn of NIST and John Padgette, Michael Zirkle, and Michael Bang of Booz Allen Hamilton for their keen and insightful assistance throughout the development of the document. The authors also greatly appreciate the feedback provided by the public comment reviewers, including Gerry Barsczewski (Social Security Administration), Mary Brown (Cisco Systems), Alex Froede (Defense Information Systems Agency [DISA]), and Tim Kramer (U.S. Navy).

Note to Readers

This document complements, and does not replace, NIST Special Publication 800-97, *Establishing Wireless Robust Security Networks: A Guide to IEEE 802.11i*, which addresses IEEE 802.11i-based WLANs. Also, the Bluetooth information and recommendations previously provided in Special Publication 800-48 have been transferred to a separate document, NIST Special Publication 800-121, *Guide to Bluetooth Security*.

Table of Contents

List of Appendices

List of Figures

List of Tables

Executive Summary

Wireless local area networks (WLAN) are groups of wireless networking nodes within a limited geographic area, such as an office building or building campus, that are capable of radio communication. WLANs are usually implemented as extensions to existing wired local area networks (LAN) to provide enhanced user mobility and network access. The most widely implemented WLAN technologies are based on the IEEE 802.11 standard and its amendments. This document discusses the security of legacy IEEE 802.11 technologies—those that are not capable of using the IEEE 802.11i security standard.

Organizations employing legacy IEEE 802.11 WLANs should be aware of the limited and weak security controls available to protect communications. Legacy WLANs are particularly susceptible to loss of confidentiality, integrity, and availability. Unauthorized users have access to well-documented security flaws and exploits that can easily compromise an organization's systems and information, corrupt the organization's data, consume network bandwidth, degrade network performance, launch attacks that prevent authorized users from accessing the network, or use the organization's resources to launch attacks on other networks.

The National Institute of Standards and Technology (NIST) recommends that organizations with existing legacy IEEE 802.11 implementations develop and implement migration strategies to move to IEEE 802.11i-based security because of its superior capabilities. IEEE 802.11i addresses the security flaws in the original IEEE 802.11 standard with built-in features providing robust wireless communications security, including support for Federal Information Processing Standard (FIPS) validated cryptographic algorithms. While legacy IEEE 802.11 networks are still in use, organizations should follow the recommendations in this publication to compensate for the security weaknesses inherent in legacy WLANs. Organizations that are planning a migration from legacy WLANs to IEEE 802.11i or are considering the deployment of new WLANs should evaluate IEEE 802.11i-based products and follow the recommendations in NIST Special Publication (SP) 800-97, *Establishing Wireless Robust Security Networks: A Guide to IEEE 802.11i*,[1] for the new WLANs.

Organizations should implement the following recommendations to improve the security of their legacy IEEE 802.11 implementations.

Organizations should be aware of the technical and security implications of legacy WLAN technologies.

Legacy WLAN technologies present unique security challenges beyond those encountered with their wired network counterparts. In addition to facing the same threats that wired networks face, legacy WLANs are also threatened by attackers that can intercept WLAN transmissions through the air. To attempt to breach a WLAN, an attacker simply needs to be within range of the wireless transmissions. Other challenges with legacy WLAN security is that legacy standards have several serious security flaws involving the authentication of clients and the protection of the confidentiality and integrity of WLAN communications. Also, the legacy WLAN standards do not define security services for auditing, authorization, replay protection, non-repudiation, and key management. Organizations cannot rely solely on the security features provided by legacy WLAN standards to secure the WLANs adequately.

---

[1]   NIST SP 800-97 is available at http://csrc.nist.gov/publications/nistpubs/800-97/SP800-97.pdf.

Organizations should create a wireless networking security policy that addresses legacy IEEE 802.11 WLAN security.

A wireless networking security policy and an organization's ability to enforce compliance with it are the foundations for all other security countermeasures. Policy considerations should include the following:

- Roles and responsibilities, such as which parties are authorized and responsible for installing and configuring WLAN equipment

- WLAN infrastructure security, including physical security requirements, acceptable use guidelines, and requirements for the use of encryption and for cryptographic key management

- WLAN client device security, such as hardware and software configuration requirements, limitations on how and when WLAN client devices may be used, and guidelines for the protection of WLAN client devices

- WLAN security assessments, particularly the frequency and scope of assessments and the actions to be taken when rogue or misconfigured devices are identified.

Organizations should be aware that physical security controls are especially important in a wireless environment.

Organizations should make sure that adequate physical security controls are in place. Additional physical security measures may be needed to protect WLAN infrastructure components dispersed throughout facilities, such as access points (AP), from theft, alteration, and misuse. Organizations should also consider the range of each AP in the context of the facilities' physical boundaries; communications that extend beyond these boundaries are susceptible to eavesdropping by external parties. Organizations concerned about eavesdropping threats should limit legacy WLAN signal propagation, at a minimum so that it does not go beyond the physical control boundaries of the organization's facilities. However, there is always a possibility that an attacker might use a high-gain antenna from a relatively long distance to eavesdrop, so only by using strong cryptographic means can any assurance of protection against eavesdropping be achieved.

Organizations needing to protect the confidentiality and integrity of their legacy WLAN communications should implement additional security controls.

The security features provided by legacy WLAN standards do not provide adequate protection for confidentiality and integrity, so additional controls are needed. One option is establishing a virtual private network (VPN) tunnel between the WLAN client device and a VPN concentrator located behind the AP. Federal agencies using VPNs to protect the confidentiality and integrity of legacy WLAN communications must configure the VPNs to use FIPS-validated encryption algorithms contained in validated cryptographic modules. WLAN management traffic often needs to be protected as well; this can be done through several methods, including using VPNs and placing the traffic on a dedicated wired network or a virtual local area network (VLAN) to isolate it from WLAN users.

Organizations should configure their legacy IEEE 802.11 APs to support the WLAN's security.

WLAN APs often have vulnerabilities and other weaknesses in their default configurations. Organizations should ensure that AP management is configured properly. This includes configuring administrator access, controlling the AP reset function, configuring network management protocols, and enabling logging. Organizations should also ensure that APs are configured to support a secure WLAN configuration. An example is changing the default channel and power output to avoid radio interference that could cause a denial of service. Also, organizations should ensure that APs are kept current with security patches, upgrades, and firmware updates to eliminate known vulnerabilities.

Organizations should properly secure their legacy IEEE 802.11 client devices to enhance the WLAN's security posture.

Securing the WLAN infrastructure without securing the client devices renders the entire WLAN insecure. Client device security considerations include using personal firewalls, host-based intrusion detection and prevention systems, and antivirus software on client devices; disabling IEEE 802.11 ad hoc mode; managing IEEE 802.11 radios, such as disabling them when not in use; and configuring client devices to comply with WLAN policies. Client devices should also be kept current with any patches or other updates related to legacy IEEE 802.11 security.

1. Introduction

1.1 Authority

The National Institute of Standards and Technology (NIST) developed this document in furtherance of its statutory responsibilities under the Federal Information Security Management Act (FISMA) of 2002, Public Law 107-347.

NIST is responsible for developing standards and guidelines, including minimum requirements, for providing adequate information security for all agency operations and assets; however, such standards and guidelines shall not apply to national security systems. This guideline is consistent with the requirements of the Office of Management and Budget (OMB) Circular A-130, Section 8b (3), "Securing Agency Information Systems," as analyzed in A-130, Appendix IV: Analysis of Key Sections. Supplemental information is provided in A-130, Appendix III.

This guideline has been prepared for use by Federal agencies. It may be used by nongovernmental organizations on a voluntary basis and is not subject to copyright, although attribution is desired.

Nothing in this document should be taken to contradict standards and guidelines made mandatory and binding on Federal agencies by the Secretary of Commerce under statutory authority, nor should these guidelines be interpreted as altering or superseding the existing authorities of the Secretary of Commerce, Director of the OMB, or any other Federal official.

1.2 Purpose and Scope

The purpose of this document is to provide guidance to organizations in securing their legacy IEEE 802.11 wireless local area networks (WLAN) that cannot use IEEE 802.11i. Details on securing WLANs capable of IEEE 802.11i can be found in NIST Special Publication (SP) 800-97. Recommendations for securely using external WLANs, such as public wireless access points, are outside the scope of this document.

1.3 Audience and Assumptions

This document covers details specific to wireless technologies and security. While it is technical in nature, it provides the necessary background to fully understand the topics that are discussed.

The following list highlights people with differing roles and responsibilities that might benefit from this document:

■ Government managers (e.g., chief information officers and senior managers) who maintain legacy IEEE 802.11 WLAN devices in their organizations

■ Systems engineers and architects who design and implement WLANs

■ System and network administrators who administer, patch, secure, or upgrade WLANs

■ Auditors, security consultants, and others who perform security assessments of WLANs

■ Researchers and analysts who are trying to understand the underlying wireless technologies.

This document assumes that the readers have at least some operating system, networking, and security knowledge. Because of the constantly changing nature of wireless networking and the threats and vulnerabilities to the technologies, readers are strongly encouraged to take advantage of other resources (including those listed in this document) for more current and detailed information.

1.4   Document Organization

The remainder of this document is composed of the following sections and appendices:

- Section 2 provides an overview of IEEE 802.11 WLAN standards, components, and architectural models.

- Section 3 discusses the basics of WLAN security.

- Section 4 examines the security capabilities provided by legacy IEEE 802.11 standards.

- Section 5 discusses threats and vulnerabilities involving legacy IEEE 802.11 WLANs.

- Section 6 explains common legacy IEEE 802.11 WLAN countermeasures and makes recommendations for their use.

- Appendix A provides a list of IEEE 802.11 WLAN standards.

- Appendix B provides a glossary of terms.

- Appendix C provides a list of acronyms and abbreviations used in this document.

- Appendix D lists legacy IEEE 802.11 WLAN references.

- Appendix E lists legacy IEEE 802.11 WLAN online resources.

2. Overview of IEEE 802.11 Wireless Local Area Networks

Wireless local area networks (WLAN) are groups of wireless networking nodes within a limited geographic area, such as an office building or building campus, that are capable of radio communication. WLANs are usually implemented as extensions to existing wired local area networks (LAN) to provide enhanced user mobility and network access. This section briefly describes several commonly used forms of WLAN technologies: IEEE 802.11a, 802.11b, 802.11g, and 802.11n. In addition, a brief overview of the updated security standard for IEEE 802.11 networks, IEEE 802.11i, is provided.

2.1 IEEE 802.11 Variants

WLAN technologies were first available in late 1990, when vendors began introducing products that operated within the 900 megahertz (MHz) frequency band. These solutions, which used non-standard, proprietary designs, provided data transfer rates of approximately 1 megabit per second (Mbps). This was significantly slower than the 10 Mbps speed provided by most wired LANs at that time. In 1992, vendors began selling WLAN products that used the 2.4 gigahertz (GHz) Industrial, Scientific, and Medical (ISM) band. Although these products provided higher data transfer rates than 900 MHz band products, they were expensive, provided relatively low data rates, were prone to radio interference, and were often designed to use proprietary radio frequency (RF) technologies.

The IEEE initiated the IEEE 802.11 project in 1990 with the objective to "develop a Medium Access Control (MAC) and Physical Layer (PHY) specification for wireless connectivity for fixed, portable, and moving stations within an area."[2] In 1997, IEEE first approved the IEEE 802.11 international interoperability standard for WLANs. The IEEE 802.11 standard supports three transmission methods, including radio transmission within the 2.4 GHz ISM band. In 1999, IEEE ratified two amendments to the IEEE 802.11 standard—IEEE 802.11a and IEEE 802.11b—that define radio transmission methods and modulation techniques. WLAN equipment based on IEEE 802.11b quickly became the dominant wireless technology. IEEE 802.11b equipment transmits in the 2.4 GHz band, offering data rates of up to 11 Mbps. IEEE 802.11b was intended to provide performance, throughput, and security features comparable to wired LANs. IEEE 802.11a operates in the 5 GHz Unlicensed National Information Infrastructure (UNII) frequency band, delivering data rates up to 54 Mbps. In 2003, IEEE released the IEEE 802.11g amendment, which specifies a radio transmission method that also uses the 2.4 GHz ISM band and can support data rates of up to 54 Mbps. In addition, IEEE 802.11g-compliant products are backward compatible with IEEE 802.11b-compliant products.

In 2006, the first IEEE 802.11n draft was introduced to enhance the range and speed of WLANs up to theoretical speeds of 300 Mbps. IEEE 802.11n maintains backward compatibility with IEEE 802.11a/b/g WLANs because it operates on both the 2.4 GHz ISM band and the 5.0 GHz UNII band. Throughput is enhanced over its predecessors by using wider bandwidth channels and devices equipped with multiple antennas to better use RF signal. In addition, IEEE 802.11n almost doubles the effective range of the WLAN.

The IEEE 802.11 variants[3] listed in Table 2-1 all include security features known collectively as Wired Equivalent Privacy (WEP), which were developed to provide a level of security comparable to that of unencrypted wired LANs. As described in Section 4, IEEE 802.11 configurations that rely on WEP have several well-documented security problems. The IEEE and the Wi-Fi Alliance acknowledged the scope

---

[2]   http://www.ieee802.org/11/Tutorial/General.pdf
[3]   For information on IEEE 802.11 and its amendments (e.g., 802.11e and 802.11n), see Appendix A, as well as
       http://grouper.ieee.org/groups/802/11/QuickGuide_IEEE_802_WG_and_Activities.htm and
       http://standards.ieee.org/getieee802.

of the problems and developed short-term and long-term strategies for rectifying the situation. In early 2003, the Wi-Fi Alliance, in coordination with the IEEE 802.11 Working Group, developed the Wi-Fi Protected Access (WPA) security enhancement to replace WEP. This was implemented as a stopgap measure until a robust IEEE 802.11 security standard could be developed and approved. In June 2004, the IEEE finalized the 802.11i amendment, which was designed to overcome the shortcomings of WEP, enhance WPA, and provide IEEE 802.11 based wireless networks with a robust security mechanism. IEEE 802.11i specifies a security framework that operates in conjunction with all the IEEE 802.11 radio transmission standards and modulation techniques, such as IEEE 802.11a, 802.11b, and 802.11g; any future IEEE 802.11 standard will also be compatible with IEEE 802.11i.[4]

Table 2-1. Summary of IEEE 802.11 WLAN Technologies

IEEE Standard or Amendment	Maximum Data Rate	Frequency Band	Comments
802.11	2 Mbps	2.4 GHz (ISM)	Legacy technology that is minimally used
802.11a	54 Mbps	5 GHz (UNII)	Not compatible with IEEE 802.11b or IEEE 802.11g Provides better than 10Base-T Ethernet speeds
802.11b	11 Mbps	2.4 GHz (ISM)	Equipment based on IEEE 802.11b has been the dominant WLAN technology Provides close to 10Base-T Ethernet speeds Is generally combined with IEEE 802.11g as product offerings as IEEE 802.11b/g
802.11g	54 Mbps	2.4 GHz (ISM)	Backward compatible with IEEE 802.11b Provides better than 10Base-T Ethernet speeds Supported by most current WLAN products
802.11n	300 Mbps	2.4 GHz (ISM) and 5 GHZ (UNII)	Backward compatible with IEEE 802.11a/b/g Provides better than 10Base-T Ethernet speeds

IEEE 802.11i includes many security enhancements that leverage mature and proven security technologies. For example, IEEE 802.11i references the use of Extensible Authentication Protocol (EAP) standards, some of which are capable of providing mutual authentication between wireless clients and the WLAN infrastructure, as well as performing automatic cryptographic key distribution. In addition, IEEE 802.11i provides means for the use of accepted cryptographic practices, such as generating cryptographic checksums through hash message authentication codes (HMAC).

The IEEE 802.11i specification introduces the concept of a Robust Security Network (RSN). RSN networks are restricted to Robust Security Network Associations (RSNA); a RSNA is a logical connection between communicating IEEE 802.11 entities established through the IEEE 802.11i key management scheme, which is called the 4-Way Handshake. The handshake is a protocol that validates that both entities share a master key, synchronizes the installation of temporal keys, and confirms the selection and configuration of data confidentiality and integrity protocols. The master key, known as the pairwise master key (PMK), serves as the basis for the IEEE 802.11i data confidentiality and integrity protocols that provide enhanced security over the flawed WEP from earlier versions of IEEE 802.11.

---

[4] In 2007, an updated version of the IEEE 802.11 standard was released (http://standards.ieee.org/getieee802/download/802.11-2007.pdf), and the IEEE 802.11i amendment and several other amendments were rolled into the main IEEE 802.11 standard. For clarity, this publication still references IEEE 802.11i because of the brevity and clarity in doing so, as opposed to referencing the corresponding sets of features within the 2007 version of the IEEE 802.11 standard.

WPA2 is the Wi-Fi Alliance interoperable specification for IEEE 802.11i. Organizations that are considering the deployment of new WLANs should evaluate IEEE 802.11i/WPA2-based products and follow the recommendations for IEEE 802.11i/WPA2 implementations presented in NIST SP 800-97, *Establishing Wireless Robust Security Networks: A Guide to IEEE 802.11i.*[5] The recommendations in NIST SP 800-97 should also be applied to existing IEEE 802.11i WLAN implementations.

2.2 IEEE 802.11 Network Components and Architectural Models

IEEE 802.11 has two fundamental architectural components:

■ **Station (STA).** A *STA* is a wireless endpoint device. Typical examples of STAs are laptop computers, PDAs, mobile telephones, and other consumer electronic devices with IEEE 802.11 capabilities.

■ **AP.**[6] An *AP* logically connects STAs with a distribution system (DS), which is typically an organization's wired infrastructure. APs can also logically connect wireless STAs with each other without accessing a DS. In addition, APs can function in a bridge mode, which allows APs to create point-to-point connections to join two separate networks.

The IEEE 802.11 standard defines two basic network topologies. The first, ad hoc mode, does not use APs—only STAs are involved in the communications. The second, infrastructure mode, has an AP that connects wireless STAs to each other or to a DS, typically a wired network. Infrastructure mode is the most commonly used mode for WLANs.

The ad hoc mode is depicted conceptually in Figure 2-1. This mode of operation, also known as *peer-to-peer mode*, is possible when two or more STAs are able to communicate directly to one another. Figure 2-1 shows three devices communicating with each other in a peer-to-peer fashion without any wireless infrastructure or wired connections. A set of STAs configured in this ad hoc manner is known as an *independent basic service set* (IBSS).

Today, a STA is most often thought of as a simple laptop computer using an inexpensive wireless network interface card (NIC) that provides wireless connectivity. As IEEE 802.11 and its variants continue to increase in popularity, many other types of devices could also be STAs, such as scanners, printers, and digital cameras. Figure 2-1 depicts a sample IBSS that includes a mobile telephone, laptop computer, and a PDA communicating via IEEE 802.11 technology. The circle in Figure 2-1 represents the signal range of the devices, which is important to consider because this determines the coverage area within which the stations can remain in communication. A fundamental property of IBSS is that it defines no routing or forwarding, so all the devices must be within radio range of one another.

---

[5]   NIST SP 800-97 is available at http://csrc.nist.gov/publications/nistpubs/800-97/SP800-97.pdf.
[6]   Technically, APs are also STAs. Some literature distinguishes between AP STAs and non-AP STAs. In this document, the term STA refers to non-AP STAs only.

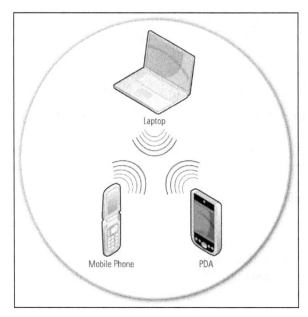

Figure 2-1. IEEE 802.11 Ad Hoc Mode Architecture

One of the key advantages of ad hoc WLANs is that theoretically they can be formed anytime and anywhere, allowing multiple users to create wireless connections cheaply, quickly, and easily with minimal hardware and user maintenance. In practice, a number of different types of ad hoc networks are possible, and the IEEE 802.11 specification allows many of them. An ad hoc network can be created for various reasons, such as supporting file sharing activities between two client devices. However, client devices operating solely in ad hoc mode cannot communicate with external wireless networks. A further complication is that an ad hoc network can interfere with the operation of an AP-based infrastructure mode network that exists within the same wireless space.

In infrastructure mode, an IEEE 802.11 WLAN comprises one or more Basic Service Sets (BSS), the basic building blocks of a WLAN. A *BSS* includes an AP and one or more STAs. The AP in a BSS connects the STAs to the DS. The DS is the means by which STAs can communicate with an organization's wired LANs and external networks, such as the Internet. The IEEE 802.11 infrastructure mode is outlined in Figure 2-2 by two BSSs connected to a DS.

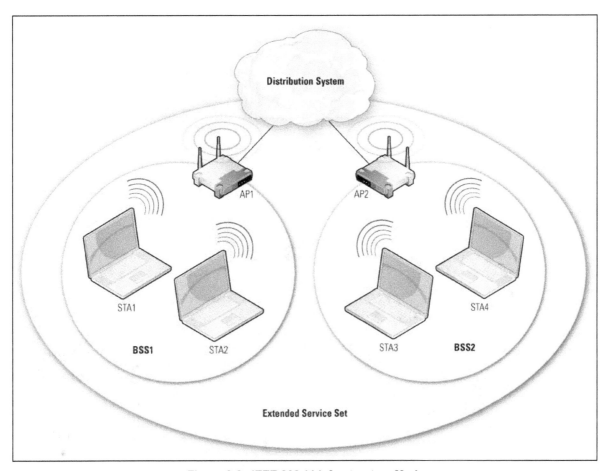

Figure 2-2. IEEE 802.11 Infrastructure Mode

The use of multiple APs connected to a single DS allows for the creation of wireless networks of arbitrary size and complexity. In the IEEE 802.11 specification, a multi-BSS network is referred to as an *extended service set* (ESS). Figure 2-3 conceptually depicts a network with both wired and wireless capabilities, similar to what would generally be deployed in an enterprise environment. It shows three APs with corresponding BSSs, which comprise an ESS. The ESS is attached to the wired enterprise network or DS, which, in turn, is connected to the Internet and other outside networks. This architecture could permit various STAs, such as laptop computers and PDAs, to access network resources and the Internet. In addition, the use of an ESS provides the opportunity for IEEE 802.11 WLAN STAs to roam between APs while maintaining network connectivity.

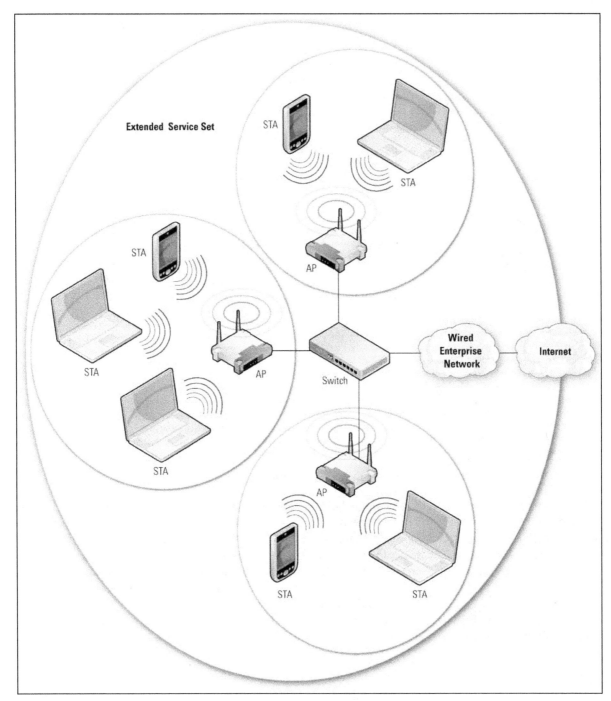

Figure 2-3. Extended Service Set in an Enterprise

2.3 Wireless Local Area Network Range and Use

The reliable coverage range for IEEE 802.11 WLANs depends on several factors, including data rate requirements and capacity, sources of RF interference, physical area characteristics, power, connectivity, and antenna usage. The typical range for connectivity of IEEE 802.11 network equipment is 50 to 100 meters (about 328 ft.) indoors, with significantly greater ranges achievable outdoors. Increased power output and special high-gain antennas can increase the range of IEEE 802.11 network devices to several miles.

APs may also provide a bridging function that connects two or more networks together and allows them to communicate via the wireless radio. Bridging involves either a point-to-point or a multipoint configuration. In a point-to-point architecture, two wired LANs are connected to each other via each LAN's wireless bridging device. In multipoint bridging, one subnet on a wired LAN is connected to several other subnets on another wired LAN via each subnet's bridging device, eliminating the need for wired links. For example, if a computer on network A needed to connect to computers on networks B, C, and D, network A's wireless bridging device would connect to B's, C's, and D's respective wireless bridging devices.

Enterprises may use bridging to connect wired LANs between different buildings on corporate campuses. Bridging devices are typically placed on top of buildings to achieve greater antenna reception. Typical bridges may extend for several miles, but may vary depending on several factors, including the specific receiver or transceiver being used, power-output, antenna type, and environmental conditions. Figure 2-4 illustrates a point-to-point wireless bridging between two wired LANs located in two separate buildings. In the example, wireless data is being transmitted from a client device in Building A to a client device in Building B, using each building's appropriately positioned bridging device to transmit and receive data between the two buildings. A client device in Building A connects to the wired enterprise network located in Building A, which then transmits any data intended for a client device in Building B over the wireless bridged link. Any data originating from a client device in Building B, intended for a client device in Building A, will be sent by Building B's wired LAN to the wireless bridging device and transmitted to Building A's wireless bridging device, which then passes the data on to Building A's wired enterprise network and finally to a client device in Building A. This sequence takes place for all data traversing the bridge link.

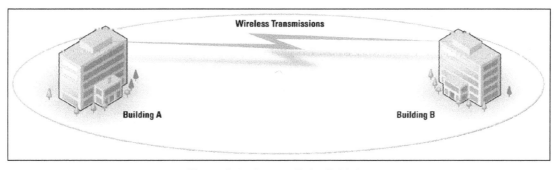

Figure 2-4. Access Point Bridging

3.   Overview of Wireless Local Area Network Security

WLAN technologies typically need to support several security objectives. The most common security objectives for WLANs are:

■ **Confidentiality**—ensure that communication cannot be read by unauthorized parties

■ **Integrity**—detect any intentional or unintentional changes to data that occur in transit

■ **Availability**—ensure that devices and individuals can access a WLAN and its resources whenever needed.

The security objectives for wireless and wired networks are the same, as are the major high-level categories of threats that they face. Table 3-1 provides a list of these categories.

Table 3-1. Major Threats Against Network Security

Threat Category	Description
Denial of Service	Attacker prevents or limits the normal use or management of networks or network devices.
Eavesdropping	Attacker passively monitors network communications for data, including authentication credentials.
Man-in-the-Middle	Attacker actively impersonates multiple legitimate parties, such as appearing as a client to an AP and appearing as an AP to a client. Allows attacker to intercept communications between an AP and a client, thereby obtaining authentication credentials and data.
Masquerading	Attacker impersonates an authorized user and gains certain unauthorized privileges.
Message Modification	Attacker alters a legitimate message by deleting, adding to, changing, or reordering it.
Message Replay	Attacker passively monitors transmissions and retransmits messages, acting as if the attacker were a legitimate user.
Misappropriation	Attacker steals or makes unauthorized use of a service.
Traffic Analysis	Attacker passively monitors transmissions to identify communication patterns and participants.

Most threats against wireless networks involve an attacker with access to the radio link between wireless devices. Several of the threats listed in Table 3-1 rely on an attacker's ability to intercept and inject network communications. This highlights the most significant difference between protecting wireless and wired networks: the relative ease of intercepting wireless network transmissions and inserting new or altered transmissions from what is presumed to be the authentic source. To breach a wired network, an attacker would have to gain physical access to the network or remotely compromise systems on the network; for a wireless network, an attacker simply needs to be within range of the wireless transmissions, making eavesdropping a particularly prevalent threat. (Some attackers use highly sensitive directional antennas, which can greatly extend the effective range of attack on the wireless networks beyond the standard range.) Another consideration in threats against wireless networks is that, in many cases, a wireless network is logically connected to a wired network, so the wireless network should be secured against both the threats that wired networks typically face and the threats that are specific to wireless networks.

In addition to eavesdropping, another common threat against wireless networks is the deployment of rogue wireless devices. For example, an attacker could deploy a wireless access point (AP) that has been configured to appear as part of an organization's wireless network infrastructure. This provides a backdoor into the wired network, bypassing perimeter security mechanisms, such as firewalls. In addition, if clients inadvertently connect to the rogue device, the attacker can view and manipulate the clients' communications.

Denial of service (DoS) situations are another threat against wireless networks. Examples are flooding (an attacker sends large numbers of messages at a high rate to prevent the wireless network from processing legitimate traffic) and jamming (a device emits electromagnetic energy on the wireless network's frequency to make it unusable). Jamming often occurs unintentionally; for example, microwave ovens, cordless telephones, and other devices share bandwidth with certain wireless technologies, and the devices' operation can inadvertently make wireless networks in proximity unusable. Denial of service conditions can also be caused through protocol manipulation, such as improper requests or responses that cause devices to enter abnormal states.

Network security attacks against WLANs are typically divided into *passive* and *active* attacks. These two broad classes are then subdivided into other types of attacks. All are defined below.

- **Passive Attack:** an attack in which an unauthorized party gains access to an asset and does not modify its content or actively attack or disrupt a WLAN. There are two types of passive attacks:

  - **Eavesdropping.** The attacker monitors wireless data transmissions between devices for message content, such as authentication credentials or passwords. An example of this attack is an attacker listening to transmissions on a WLAN between an AP and a client.

  - **Traffic analysis** (also known as traffic flow analysis). The attacker gains intelligence by monitoring the transmissions for patterns of communication. A considerable amount of information is contained in the flow of messages between communicating parties. This is a more subtle method than eavesdropping.

- **Active Attack:** an attack whereby an unauthorized party makes modifications to a message, data stream, or file. It is possible to detect this type of attack, but it may not be preventable. Active attacks may take the form of one of four types (or a combination thereof):

  - **Masquerading.** The attacker impersonates an authorized user to gain access to certain unauthorized privileges.

  - **Replay.** The attacker monitors transmissions (passive attack) and retransmits messages posing as the legitimate user.

  - **Message modification.** The attacker alters a legitimate message by deleting, adding to, changing, or reordering the message.

  - **DoS.** The attacker prevents or prohibits the normal use or management of a WLAN.

4. Security of Legacy IEEE 802.11 WLAN Standards

This section describes the security features provided by legacy IEEE 802.11 WLAN standards and explains their limitations. The section addresses WEP[7] and WPA, which are designed to protect link-level data during wireless transmission between clients and APs. As Figure 4-1 shows, WLAN standards cannot provide end-to-end security because they are only used for the wireless link between the AP and STA.

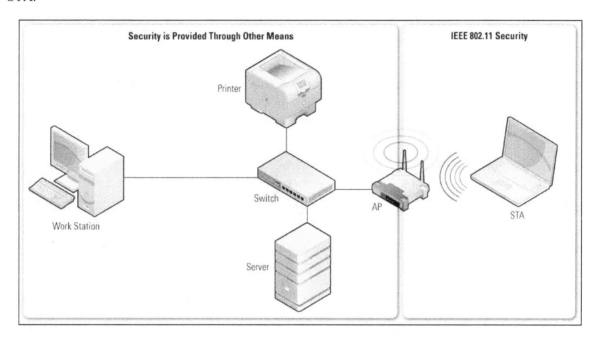

Figure 4-1. Lack of End-to-End Security from WLAN Security Features

WEP, which is now known to have a number of security vulnerabilities, was designed by the IEEE to provide the following three basic security services:

■ **Authentication:** to verify the identity of communicating client stations. This controls access to the network by denying access to client stations that cannot authenticate properly.

■ **Confidentiality:** to use encryption to provide wireless networks with the same or similar privacy achieved by an unencrypted wired network. The intent was to prevent information compromise from casual eavesdropping.

■ **Integrity:** to ensure that messages were not modified in transit between wireless clients and APs.

WEP's intended capabilities for providing authentication and protecting confidentiality and integrity are described below, along with known weaknesses in those capabilities. It is important to note that WEP does not address other security services such as audit, authorization, replay protection, non-repudiation, and key management. The lack of key management services is particularly problematic, necessitating that organizations deploying legacy WLANs determine how to generate, distribute, store, load, escrow, archive, audit, and destroy WEP keys. Many organizations choose not to change WEP keys regularly,

---

[7]   IEEE 802.11 specifies an optional privacy algorithm, WEP, that is designed to satisfy the goal of wired LAN "equivalent" privacy. The algorithm is not designed for ultimate security but rather to be "at least as secure as a wire." Source ANSI/IEEE Std 802.11, 1999 Edition (R2003).

which provides attackers with the opportunity to capture enough data to compute the WEP key and use it to gain unauthorized access to data or perform other attacks. Many organizations also choose to use the same key for many devices, which poses a significant risk if an attacker gains access to one of the devices (for example, a laptop being lost, stolen, or infected with an attacker's malware). Using the same key for many devices also makes it easier for an attacker to perform analytic attacks to recover the key.

Also, without proper key management practices, legacy IEEE 802.11 WLANs may have key-related vulnerabilities such as the use of non-unique keys, factory default keys, or other weak keys (e.g., all zeroes, all ones, and other easily guessed patterns).

4.1 Authentication

In the legacy IEEE 802.11 specification, authentication between clients and APs is only one way: authenticating the client to the AP. The client must trust that it is communicating to a legitimate, benign AP. The legacy specification defines two authentication methods: open-system and shared-key. Open-system authentication is the only authentication method that the legacy IEEE 802.11 specification requires products to support. However, open-system authentication is not truly authentication; the AP accepts the client without verifying its identity, simply by the client providing a MAC address to the AP. There is no validation that this MAC address is not spoofed or that the client is authorized to have access, so open-system authentication is highly vulnerable to attack and practically invites unauthorized access.

The other authentication method in the legacy specification, shared-key authentication, is a cryptographic technique for authentication. It is a simple "challenge-response" scheme based on whether a client has knowledge of a shared secret—the WEP key. In this scheme, as depicted in Figure 4-2, a random challenge is generated by the AP and sent to the client in plaintext. The client then generates a pseudorandom series of bytes known as the *key stream* that is XORed[8] with the AP's plaintext challenge and sent back to the AP as an encrypted response. The AP decrypts the result computed by the client and allows access only if the decrypted value is the same as the random challenge transmitted. The algorithm used in the cryptographic computation and for the generation of the 128-bit challenge text is the RC4 stream cipher, which is not FIPS-approved.

In shared-key authentication, the initial exchange of the plaintext challenge from the AP and the encrypted response from the client is a major security design flaw. An eavesdropping attack would capture both the AP's plaintext challenge and the client's encrypted response, thereby providing an attacker with two of the three components required to determine the random key stream. An attacker can XOR the encrypted response and the plaintext challenge to determine the random key stream, thus enabling the attacker to authenticate to the AP.

If a legacy WLAN is limited to WEP authentication methods and employing WEP data encryption, open-system authentication is technically more secure than shared-key authentication because shared-key authentication can actually help facilitate an attack on the WEP encryption keys. However, neither authentication method provides any true assurance of authentication, so organizations that want to authenticate their legacy WLAN clients should consider separate authentication solutions and plan migration to WLANs using IEEE 802.11i, which support multiple strong authentication options.

---

[8] XOR, or Exclusive OR, is when the bits of two bytes are compared to generate one resulting byte. If the corresponding bits in the original two bytes are different, the resulting byte's corresponding value will be a one, if they are the same, the value will be a zero. For example, XORing a byte with value 11101001 with another byte with value 00100110 will result in the resulting byte value of 11001111.

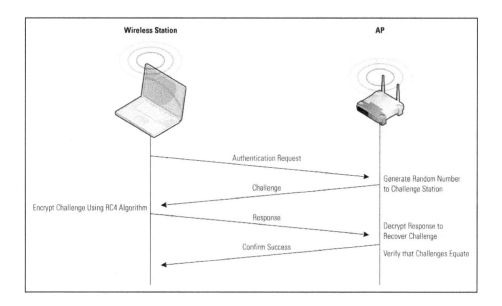

Figure 4-2. Shared-Key Authentication Message Flow

4.2 Confidentiality

WEP employs the RC4 stream cipher algorithm to encrypt wireless communications to protect transmitted data from disclosure to eavesdroppers. The standard for WEP specifies support for a 40-bit WEP key only; many vendors offer non-standard extensions to WEP that support key lengths of up to 104 or even 232 bits. WEP also uses a 24-bit value known as an initialization vector (IV) as a seed value for initializing the cryptographic key stream. For example, a 104-bit WEP key with a 24-bit IV becomes a 128-bit RC4 key. Ideally, larger key sizes translate to stronger protection, but the cryptographic technique used by WEP has known flaws that are not mitigated by longer keys because the key flaws are a result of the weak implementation of the IV and RC4 symmetric-key, stream cipher algorithm. WEP is applied to all data above the IEEE 802.11 WLAN layers to protect traffic such as Transmission Control Protocol/Internet Protocol (TCP/IP), Internet Packet Exchange (IPX), and Hypertext Transfer Protocol (HTTP). WEP is illustrated conceptually in Figure 4-3.

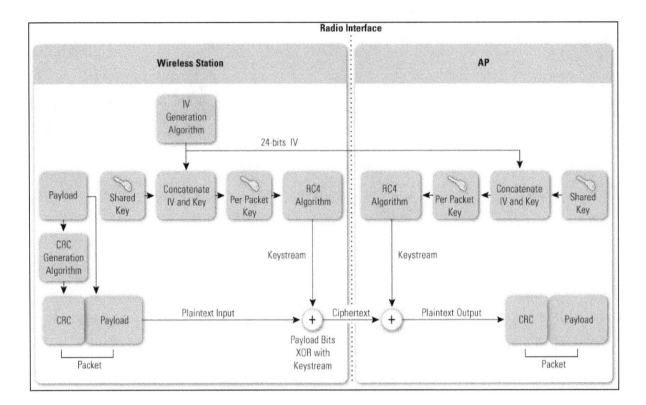

Figure 4-3. WEP Using RC4 Algorithm

Most attacks against WEP encryption have been based on IV-related vulnerabilities. The IV portion of the RC4 key is sent in cleartext, allowing an eavesdropper to monitor and analyze a relatively small amount of network traffic to recover the key by taking advantage of the IV value knowledge, the relatively small 24-bit IV key space, and a weakness in the way WEP implements the RC4 algorithm. Also, WEP does not specify precisely how the IVs should be set or changed, so some products use a static, well-known IV value or reset the IV to zero. If two messages have the same IV, and the plaintext of either message is known, it is relatively trivial for an attacker to determine the plaintext of the other message. In particular, because many messages contain common protocol headers or other easily decipherable contents, it is often possible to identify the original plaintext contents with minimal effort. Even traffic from products that use sequentially increasing IV values is still susceptible to attack. There are fewer than 17 million possible IV values; on a busy WLAN, the entire IV space may be exhausted in a few hours. When the IV is chosen randomly, which represents the best possible generic IV selection algorithm, by the birthday paradox, two IVs already have a 50% chance of repeating after about 2^{12} (or 4,096) frames.

Another possible threat to confidentiality is network traffic analysis. Eavesdroppers might be able to gain information by monitoring which parties communicate at what times. Also, analyzing traffic patterns can aid in determining the content of communications; for example, short bursts of activity might be caused by terminal emulation or instant messaging, while steady streams of activity might be generated by video conferencing. More sophisticated analysis might be able to determine the operating systems in use based on the length of certain frames. Other than encrypting communications, the legacy IEEE 802.11 standard, like most other network protocols, does not offer any features that might thwart network traffic analysis, such as adding random lengths of padding to messages or sending additional messages with randomly generated data.

Some legacy WLAN devices can be upgraded through firmware to support WPA. WPA includes two main features: IEEE 802.1X and the Temporal Key Integrity Protocol (TKIP). The IEEE 802.1X port-based access control provides a framework to allow the use of robust upper-layer authentication protocols. It also facilitates the use of session keys that allow the rotation of cryptographic keys. TKIP includes four new features to enhance the security of IEEE 802.11: TKIP extends the IV space, allows for per-packet key construction, provides cryptographic integrity, and provides key derivation and distribution. Through these features, TKIP provides protection against various security attacks discussed earlier, including replay attacks and attacks on data integrity. In addition, it addresses the critical need to periodically change encryption keys. However, WPA has significant flaws and does not provide the level of security that IEEE 802.11i can.[9] Table 4-1 below outlines the various IEEE 802.11 wireless security standards. Of the four security methods shown in the table, it is important to note that only Counter Mode with Cipher Block Chaining MAC Protocol (CCMP) RSN, which is used by IEEE 802.11i, has a cryptographic algorithm that is FIPS-validated. WEP and WPA only use cryptographic algorithms that do not meet the requirements for FIPS 140-2 validation.

Table 4-1. Summary of Data Confidentiality and Integrity Protocols

Security Feature	Manual WEP (pre-RSN)	Dynamic WEP (pre-RSN)	TKIP (RSN)	CCMP (RSN)
Core cryptographic algorithm	RC4	RC4	RC4	AES
Key sizes	40-bit or 104-bit (encryption)	40-bit or 104-bit (encryption)	128-bit (encryption), 64-bit (integrity protection)	128-bit (encryption and integrity protection)
Per-packet key	Created through concatenation of WEP key and the 24-bit IV	Derived from EAP authentication	Created through TKIP mixing function	Not needed; temporal key is sufficiently secure
Integrity mechanism	Enciphered CRC-32	Enciphered CRC-32	Michael message integrity check (MIC) with countermeasures	CCM
Header protection	None	None	Source and destination addresses protected by Michael MIC	Source and destination addresses protected by CCM
Replay detection	None	None	Enforce IV sequencing	Enforce IV sequencing
Authentication	Open system or shared key	EAP method with IEEE 802.1X	EAP method with IEEE 802.1X or PSK	EAP method with IEEE 802.1X or PSK
Key distribution	Manual	IEEE 802.1X	IEEE 802.1X or manual	IEEE 802.1X or manual

4.3 Integrity

WEP supports data integrity by checking messages transmitted between STAs and APs. WEP is designed to reject any messages that have been changed in transit, such as by a man-in-the-middle attack. WEP data integrity is based on a simple encrypted checksum—a 32-bit cyclic redundancy check (CRC-32) computed on each payload prior to transmission. The payload and checksum are encrypted using the RC4 key stream before transmission. The receiver decrypts each transmission, recomputes the checksum on

---

[9] The objective of WPA was to bring a standards-based interim security solution to the marketplace to replace WEP until IEEE developed a new wireless security specification (IEEE 802.11i).

the received payload, and compares it with the transmitted checksum. If the checksums are not the same, the transmitted data frame has been altered in transit, and the frame is discarded.

Unfortunately, the WEP integrity scheme is vulnerable to certain attacks regardless of key size because its simple CRC is not a "cryptographically secure" mechanism such as a cryptographic hash or message authentication code. The CRC-32 is subject to a number of security threats, including bit-flipping attacks, which occur when an attacker knows which CRC-32 bits will change when message bits are altered. WEP attempts to counter this problem by encrypting the CRC-32 to produce an Integrity Check Value (ICV). While the creators of WEP believed that an encrypted CRC-32 would be more resistant to tampering, they did not realize that a property of stream ciphers such as WEP's RC4 is that bit flipping survives the encryption process—the same bits flip whether or not encryption is used. Therefore, the WEP ICV offers no additional protection against bit flipping. Cryptographic checksums prevent bit flipping attacks because they are designed so that any change to the original message results in significant and unpredictable changes to the resulting checksum.

4.4   Recommendations

WEP has several significant security problems, most of which cannot be solved by reconfiguration of WEP itself. For example, increasing the length of the WEP key would only marginally increase the time needed to decrypt packets. WEP does not provide an acceptable level of wireless transmission security, so it should not be the sole security mechanism used in legacy IEEE 802.11 WLAN deployments. More robust WLAN security solutions, such as those outlined in NIST SP 800-97,[10] or compensating controls should be implemented to provide the needed security. Because of the serious security flaws in the legacy IEEE 802.11 standard, NIST recommends that organizations with existing legacy IEEE 802.11 WLAN implementations develop and implement migration strategies to move to IEEE 802.11i, which offers better security.

---

[10]   NIST SP 800-97, *Establishing Wireless Robust Security Networks: A Guide to IEEE 802.11i* is available at http://csrc.nist.gov/publications/nistpubs/800-97/SP800-97.pdf.

5. Threats and Vulnerabilities

As the number of organizations that deploy wireless networks continues to grow, it becomes even more important to understand the types of vulnerabilities and threats facing legacy IEEE 802.11 WLANs and implement appropriate security measures. Some of the vulnerabilities that are described in this section are inherent in the legacy IEEE 802.11 WLAN standard, while others are relevant to WLANs or wireless networking in general.

5.1 Loss of Confidentiality

Because of the broadcast and radio nature of wireless technology, ensuring confidentiality is significantly more difficult in a wireless network than a wired network. Traditional wired networks provide inherent security through the use of a physical medium to which an attacker needs to gain access. Wireless networks propagate signals into space, making traditional physical security countermeasures less effective and access to the network much easier, increasing the importance of adequate confidentiality on wireless networks.

Passive eavesdropping on legacy IEEE 802.11 WLAN communications may cause significant risk to an organization. An adversary can scan RF signals and capture data traversing the wireless medium. Sensitive information, including proprietary information, network IDs and passwords, and configuration data, are some examples of data that may be captured. In addition, attackers with high-gain antennas can capture data from wireless networks beyond a network's normal operating range, again making confidentiality a critical security measure.

Eavesdropping performed with a wireless network analyzer tool or *sniffer* is particularly easy for legacy IEEE 802.11 WLANs. Sniffers can take advantage of flaws in the key-scheduling algorithm that was provided for the implementation of RC4 used by WEP. To exploit these weaknesses, the sniffer passively monitors the WLAN and computes the encryption keys after a variable number of packets have been sniffed. On a highly saturated network, collecting the amount of data required to compute the WEP keys only takes several hours; if traffic volume is low, it may take up to one day. For example, a busy AP that is transmitting 3,000 bytes at 11 Mbps will exhaust the 24-bit IV space after approximately 10 hours.[11] Once the attacker recovers two ciphertexts that have used the same IV, both data integrity and confidentiality may be easily compromised. Advanced tools use methods to exploit the weakness in IEEE 802.11 security in less time. After the network packets have been received, the fundamental keys may be guessed in less than one second.[12] Once the malicious user knows the WEP key, he or she can read any packet traveling over the WLAN.

Another risk to WLANs is loss of confidentiality through simple eavesdropping on broadcast traffic. Ethernet hubs generally broadcast network traffic to all physical interfaces and connected devices, which leaves the broadcasted traffic vulnerable to unauthorized monitoring. For example, an AP connected to a port on an Ethernet hub that is broadcasting data traffic would broadcast all of the data traffic it received on its wired interface over its wireless interface. The use of the Ethernet hub infrastructure increases the risk that the AP may be broadcasting proprietary or sensitive data that was transmitted through the hub. Switches alleviate this concern by providing dedicated channels between communication devices.

A malicious or irresponsible user could surreptitiously physically insert a rogue AP into a closet, under a conference room table, or in any other hidden area within a building. The rogue AP could then be used to allow unauthorized individuals to gain access to an enterprise network. As long as its location is in close

---

[11] 10 hours = (3,000 bytes x ((8 bits/byte) / (11 x 106 bits/sec)) x 24) = 36,600 seconds)
[12] For more information from AirSnort, visit its Web page at http://airsnort.shmoo.com/.

proximity to the users of the WLAN, and it is configured to appear as a legitimate AP to wireless clients, the rogue AP may successfully convince wireless clients of its legitimacy and cause wireless clients to connect and transmit traffic to the rogue AP. In this scenario, an attacker can easily capture all of the data transmitted through the rogue AP, bypassing all wireless protocol confidentiality. It is also important to note that not all rogue APs are deployed by malicious users. In many cases, rogue APs are deployed by users who want to take advantage of wireless technology without the approval of the IT department. These APs are often deployed without proper security configurations and pose significant security risks.

5.2   Loss of Integrity

Data integrity issues in wireless networks are similar to those in wired networks. Because organizations frequently implement wireless and wired communications without adequate cryptographic protection of data, integrity can be difficult to achieve. For example, an attacker can compromise data integrity by deleting or modifying the data in an email via the wireless system. This can be detrimental to an organization if important email is widely distributed among email recipients. Because the security features of the legacy IEEE 802.11 standard do not provide strong message integrity, other kinds of active attacks that compromise system integrity are possible. The specific weaknesses of the CRC-32 integrity mechanism portion of WEP are outlined in Section 4.3.

5.3   Loss of Availability

A denial of WLAN availability often involves some form of DoS attack, such as jamming or flooding. *Jamming* occurs when an RF signal emitted from a wireless device overwhelms other wireless devices and signals, causing a loss of communications. Jamming may be caused deliberately by a malicious user or caused inadvertently by emissions from other legitimate devices operating within unlicensed spectrum, such as a cordless telephone or microwave oven. *Flooding* attacks are initiated using software designed to transmit a large number of packets to an AP or other wireless device, causing the device to be overwhelmed by packets and cease normal operation. Flooding can cause a WLAN to degrade to an unacceptable performance level or even fail completely. Jamming and flooding threats are difficult to counter in any radio-based communications, and the legacy IEEE 802.11 standard does not provide any defense against them.

IEEE 802.11 management frames provide another vector for DoS attacks against WLANs. Management frames govern the process of associating and disassociating APs and STAs from a WLAN. By design, the IEEE 802.11 standard does not provide protection against these attacks. If an adversary forges a disassociation frame and sends it to an AP or STA, the targeted device will grant the request and close its communications association. Another type of attack, known as an association attack, targets an AP's association table, which monitors the state of STAs associated with the AP. An association attack typically floods this table with false requests until the AP no longer allows legitimate associations. More advanced association attacks can force STAs to connect to false APs where the victim is subject to a variety of malicious attacks.

Another threat to legacy IEEE 802.11 WLAN availability is the use of IEEE 802.11n WLANs. IEEE 802.11n offers a Greenfield mode that disables IEEE 802.11n's backward compatibility and requires that all WLAN devices run in native IEEE 802.11n mode. Greenfield mode can cause significant interference for all non-IEEE 802.11n devices within its transmission area. For example, a neighboring IEEE 802.11n WLAN operating in Greenfield mode can unintentionally create a potential DoS for the legacy WLAN.

Users can also cause a loss of unavailability by unintentionally monopolizing the capacity of a WLAN, such as downloading large files, effectively denying other users access to the network.

6.   WLAN Security Countermeasures

Organizations should mitigate risks to their legacy IEEE 802.11 WLANs by applying countermeasures to address specific threats and vulnerabilities. Because of the security weaknesses inherent in legacy IEEE 802.11 WLANs, most of these countermeasures cannot be achieved through security features built into legacy IEEE 802.11 standards. This section describes management, operational, and technical countermeasures that can be effective in reducing the risks commonly associated with legacy IEEE 802.11 WLANs. These countermeasures do not guarantee a secure WLAN environment and cannot prevent all adversary penetrations. Also, security comes at a cost—financial expenses related to security equipment, inconvenience, maintenance, and operation. Each organization needs to evaluate the acceptable level of risk based on numerous factors, which will affect the level of security implemented by that organization. To be effective, WLAN security should be incorporated throughout the entire life cycle of WLAN solutions.[13]

FIPS Publication (PUB) 199 establishes three security categories—low, moderate, and high—based on the potential impact of a security breach involving a particular system. NIST SP 800-53 provides recommendations for minimum management, operational, and technical security controls for information systems based on the FIPS PUB 199 impact categories.[14] The recommendations in NIST SP 800-53 should be helpful to organizations in identifying controls that are needed to protect WLANs in general, which should be used in addition to the specific recommendations for legacy IEEE 802.11 WLANs listed in this document.

6.1   Management Countermeasures

Organizations should create a wireless networking security policy that addresses legacy IEEE 802.11 WLAN security. Such a policy and an organization's ability to enforce compliance with it are the foundations for all other countermeasures. Policy considerations for legacy IEEE 802.11 WLANs should include the following:

■ Roles and responsibilities

- Which users or groups of users are and are not authorized to use organization WLANs

- Which parties are authorized and responsible for installing and configuring APs and other WLAN equipment

■ WLAN infrastructure security

- Physical security requirements for WLANs and WLAN devices, including limitations on the service areas of WLANs

- Types of information that may and may not be sent over WLANs, including acceptable use guidelines

- How WLAN transmissions should be protected, including requirements for the use of encryption and for cryptographic key management

---

[13] For more information about technology life cycles, see NIST SP 800-64, *Security Considerations in the Information System Development Life Cycle* (http://csrc.nist.gov/publications/PubsSPs html).

[14] FIPS PUB 199, *Standards for Security Categorization of Federal Information and Information Systems*, is available at http://csrc.nist.gov/publications/fips/fips199/FIPS-PUB-199-final.pdf. NIST SP 800-53 Revision 2, *Recommended Security Controls for Federal Information Systems*, is available at http://csrc nist.gov/publications/nistpubs/800-53-Rev2/sp800-53-rev2-final.pdf.

■ WLAN client device security

- The conditions under which WLAN client devices are and are not allowed to be used and operated

- Standard hardware and software configurations that must be implemented on WLAN client devices to ensure the appropriate level of security

- Limitations on how and when WLAN clients device may be used, such as specific locations

- Guidelines on reporting losses of WLAN client devices and reporting WLAN security incidents

- Guidelines for the protection of WLAN client devices to reduce theft

■ WLAN security assessments

- The frequency and scope of WLAN security assessments

- The actions to be taken to address rogue or misconfigured devices that are identified.

Security assessments, or audits, are an essential tool for checking the security posture of a legacy IEEE 802.11 WLAN and for determining corrective action to make sure such WLANs remain secure.[15] It is important for organizations to perform regular audits using wireless sniffers and other tools.[16] Assessors, such as security administrators or auditors, can use sniffers to determine whether wireless products are transmitting correctly and on the correct channels. Assessors should periodically check within the office building space (and campus) for rogue APs and other unauthorized access. Organizations may also consider using an independent third party to conduct the security audits from an impartial perspective. In some cases, compared to an organization's own staff, a third party that specializes in wireless security may be more up-to-date on security vulnerabilities and better equipped to assess the security of a WLAN. A third-party assessment, which may include penetration testing, will help an organization ensure that its WLANs are compliant with established security procedures and policies.[17] In addition to ensuring that the wireless portion of the network is secure, organizations should also confirm the security of the wired portion.

Other recommendations for management countermeasures are as follows:

■ Consider designating an individual to track the progress of IEEE 802.11 security standards, features, threats, and vulnerabilities. This helps to ensure the continued secure implementation of WLAN technology.

■ Maintain an inventory of legacy IEEE 802.11 APs and connecting devices. This inventory is useful when conducting audits of IEEE 802.11 technologies, particularly in identifying rogue devices.

6.2   Operational Countermeasures

Physical security is fundamental for ensuring that only authorized users have access to WLAN equipment. Physical security combines such measures as access controls, personnel identification, and external boundary protection. For example, photo identification, card badge readers, or biometric devices

---

[15]   For more information on network security, see NIST SP 800-115 (Draft), *Technical Guide to Information Security Testing* (http://csrc.nist.gov/publications/PubsSPs.html).

[16]   Some WIDPS sensors are mobile and have capabilities such that they can be used to perform WLAN audits.

[17]   See "Clinic: What are the biggest security risks associated with Wireless technology? What do I need to consider if my organization wants to introduce this kind of technology to my corporate LAN?", 2001, at http://www.itsecurity.com/.

can be used to reduce the risk of improper physical penetration of facilities containing WLAN equipment. External boundary protection can include locking doors and installing video cameras for surveillance around the perimeter of a site to discourage unauthorized access to WLAN components, such as APs, from outside the organization's facilities. In addition, additional security mechanisms should be put in place if necessary to prevent the theft, alteration, or misuse of WLAN infrastructure components, such as APs, which are often dispersed throughout facilities.

It is important to consider the RF range of each AP in a legacy IEEE 802.11 WLAN. If the range extends beyond the physical boundaries of the organization's facilities, the extension creates a security vulnerability. An individual outside the facilities could eavesdrop on network communications by using a wireless device to capture wireless signals and data. A similar consideration applies to the implementation of building-to-building bridges. Ideally, the APs or bridges should be placed strategically within a building so that the range does not exceed the physical perimeter of the building and allow unauthorized personnel to eavesdrop near the perimeter.

Organizations can use site survey tools to measure the range of AP devices, both inside and outside the facilities where the WLAN is located. Such tools measure and evaluate a number of WLAN characteristics, including signal strength, range, data rate, and other factors. These measurements can be used to map out the appropriate coverage area, capacity, and data rates for required WLAN usage. A proper site survey can help ensure that signals for WLAN deployments do not extend beyond the appropriate service area to unrestricted areas, such as parking lots or public areas.[18] Although mapping the coverage area is helpful with regard to security, it is not an absolute solution. There is always a possibility that an attacker might use a high-gain antenna from a relatively long distance to eavesdrop on the WLAN traffic. Only by using strong cryptographic means can a user gain any assurance of protection against eavesdropping adversaries.

Organizations concerned about eavesdropping threats should limit legacy WLAN signal propagation, at a minimum so that it does not go beyond the physical control boundaries of the organization's facilities. There are various ways to meet RF containment goals, with the easiest being selecting proper antenna types and setting appropriate power settings. For example, if the coverage area is a conference room, setting the antenna's power amplification to full power would not be necessary. Many tools can predict RF propagation by calculating coverage distance based on antenna type and power input. Power configuration settings can be changed in most APs' management consoles. In addition, choosing the right kinds of antennas can assist with signal containment. For example, when appropriate, using wall-mounted antennas that propagate signal at 180 degrees or less can minimize signal leakage.

Additional recommendations for operational countermeasures involve training and awareness. Organizations should ensure that users of legacy IEEE 802.11 WLANs are properly trained on their secure use. Also, network administrators should be fully aware of the security risks that WLANs and wireless devices pose. They should work to ensure security policy compliance and be aware of the steps to take in the event of a WLAN-related security incident.

6.3 Technical Countermeasures

Technical countermeasures involve the use of hardware and software solutions to help secure the legacy WLAN environment. The following subsections discuss possible countermeasures for legacy WLANs and make recommendations for their use.

---

[18] One method of controlling WLAN signals involves the use of directional antennas to control RF emanations. Directional antennas do not protect network links; they merely help control coverage range by limiting signal dispersion.

6.3.1 Confidentiality and Integrity Protection

WPA was designed as the interim solution between WEP and the ratification of IEEE 802.11i. WPA is an upgrade to existing WEP-enabled equipment to provide a higher level of security, primarily through the use of TKIP and MIC. TKIP uses the same mechanisms as WEP to provide encryption, but TKIP provides a higher level of security because it uses a 128-bit encryption key, as opposed to the 40-bit WEP key, and it creates a new key for each packet (WEP encryption keys do not change). Also, using TKIP with MIC provides stronger integrity checking than using WEP with CRC because MIC uses a stronger cryptographic algorithm than CRC. However, it is important to note that TKIP is not FIPS-approved. Therefore, if an organization needs to protect the confidentiality and integrity of its legacy WLAN communications, it needs to employ additional security controls.

An alternative method of achieving confidentiality and integrity protection is using a virtual private network (VPN). A VPN is a virtual network, built on top of existing physical networks, that can provide a secure communications mechanism for data and IP information transmitted between networks. VPNs are often used to facilitate the secure transfer of sensitive data across public networks, such as the Internet, for remote access, telework, and other situations involving connecting multiple locations. VPNs can also be established within a single network, such as a WLAN, to protect sensitive communications from other parties on the network. A variety of VPN technologies exist, such as Internet Protocol Security (IPsec) VPNs and Secure Sockets Layer (SSL) VPNs. Federal agencies using VPNs to protect the confidentiality of WLAN communications must configure the VPNs to use FIPS-validated encryption algorithms contained in validated cryptographic modules.[19]

One way to use VPNs to protect WLAN communications is to establish a VPN tunnel between the WLAN client device and a VPN concentrator that is behind the AP. With an IPsec VPN, security services are provided at the network layer of the protocol stack, which will secure all applications and protocols operating at layer 3 and above. The VPN security services are independent of layer 2 wireless security and are recommended to be used if the underlying wireless security mechanisms, such as WEP, are weak. As a defense-in-depth strategy, if a VPN is in place, an organization can consider applying both VPN security and wireless security.[20] It is important to understand that VPNs do not eliminate all risk from wireless networking.

Organizations should also ensure that their WLAN management traffic's confidentiality and integrity is protected properly. This can be done through the methods described above, such as VPNs. Another option is to place the WLAN management traffic on a dedicated wired network or a virtual local area network (VLAN) to isolate it from WLAN users. This option also supports WLAN management communications when a denial of service is occurring to the wireless network.

When determining how confidentiality and integrity should be protected, organizations should review their WLAN client devices to determine the types of cryptographic algorithms that can be used, along with key lengths and their re-keying period. Secret keys should be replaced periodically to reduce the potential impact of a key compromise.

6.3.2 Wireless Intrusion Detection and Prevention Systems

A wireless intrusion detection and prevention system (WIDPS) is an effective tool for determining whether unauthorized users or devices are attempting to access, have already accessed, or have compromised a WLAN. WIDPS can also detect misconfigured WLAN clients, rogue APs, ad hoc

---

[19] More specific information and guidance on IPSec VPNs is available in NIST SP 800-77, *Guide to IPSec VPNs,* which is available at http://csrc.nist.gov/publications/PubsSPs.html.
[20] See "Identifying the Weakest Link," *Wireless Internet Magazine*, November/December 2001

networks, and other possible violations of an organization's WLAN policy.[21] Organizations with WLANs should consider implementing WIDPS solutions.[22]

The introduction of IEEE 802.11n introduces new implications for WIDPS. Because IEEE 802.11n uses both 20 MHz and 40 MHz channels, the WIDPS needs to dedicate more time to channel hopping and less time to scanning each individual channel. This change in security posture weakens the WIDPS' ability to identify attacks while they are occurring.[23] In addition, WIDPSs that have not been updated to recognize IEEE 802.11n may report their APs as being rogue or fail to detect them.

In some environments, WIDPS sensors have an additional function: *RF insertion*, which is transmitting interference traffic to increase the difficulty of WEP cracking. RF insertion does not prevent WEP cracking—it only deters novice attackers from cracking WEP with common tools by increasing the amount of traffic an attacker has to sift through. An advanced attacker can fingerprint and filter insertion packets, negating the intended effect of RF insertion. Accordingly, RF insertion provides little, if any, protection for WLANs, while also reducing WLAN throughput.

6.3.3 Access Point Configuration

Organizations should configure their legacy IEEE 802.11 APs in accordance with established security policies and requirements. APs can be categorized as thick or thin. A *thick* or *intelligent AP* handles encryption and the overall management of the client devices connected to it. For a *thin AP,* the processing of encryption and policy settings generally occurs in the central switch or controller. Thin APs are generally more secure than thick APs because thin APs do not have a key that could be extracted and also do not require the same level of physical security and other countermeasures than thick APs.

APs often have vulnerabilities and other weaknesses in their default configurations. Security considerations for APs are described below, grouped into two categories: AP management and WLAN configuration.

6.3.3.1 AP management

- **Configuring administrator access.** Each AP has its own default settings, some of which inherently contain security vulnerabilities. For example, on some APs the default configuration does not require a password or the default password is commonly known, allowing unauthorized users to easily gain access. AP default settings should be changed to reflect the organization's security policy, such as requiring strong administrator passwords (for example, a policy might require an alphanumeric and special character string at least eight characters in length).[24] In addition, the AP should lock the login screen after a specific number of failed attempts have occurred, and the AP should log out administrators automatically after a defined period of inactivity. Also, it is important to ensure that

---

[21]   Eavesdropping and other passive techniques cannot be identified by WIDPS technologies.
[22]   For more information about WIDPS, see NIST SP 800-94, *Guide to Intrusion Detection and Prevention Systems,* which is available at http://csrc.nist.gov/publications/PubsSPs.html.
[23]   It is expected that this will be a problem primarily for early adoptions of IEEE 802.11n and that future WIDPSs will adjust to this change.
[24]   An alternative to password authentication is two-factor authentication. One form of two-factor authentication uses a symmetric key algorithm to generate a new code every minute. This code is a one-time use code that is paired with the user's personal identification number (PIN) for authentication. Another example of two-factor authentication is pairing the user's smart card with the user's PIN. This type of authentication requires a hardware device reader for the smart card or an authentication server for the PIN. While several commercial products provide this capability, use of an automated password generator or two-factor authentication mechanism may not be worth the investment, depending on the organization's security requirements, number of users, and budget constraints.

communications with the management interface have the proper cryptographic protection to prevent the unauthorized disclosure of sensitive information.

■ **Controlling the reset function.** An AP's reset function may allow an individual to negate any security settings that administrators have configured in the AP. A specific type of reset will return the AP to its default factory settings. The default settings generally do not require an administrative password, for example, and may disable encryption. On some devices, an individual can reset an AP simply by inserting a pointed object such as a pen into the reset hole and pressing. A malicious user can exploit the reset feature to cancel out any security settings on the device. The reset function, if configured to erase basic operational information such as IP address or keys, can also result in a network DoS. Having physical access controls in place to prevent unauthorized users from resetting APs can mitigate the threats. In addition, resets can be invoked remotely over the management interface on some products. For this reason, it is imperative to have proper authentication and encryption on the management interface.

■ **Using SNMPv3.** Some APs use Simple Network Management Protocol (SNMP) agents, which allow network management software tools to monitor the status of APs and clients. If SNMP is not required for the WLAN, it should be disabled;[25] otherwise, SNMPv3, which includes mechanisms to provide strong security, is highly recommended over the earlier versions of SNMP.[26] SNMPv1 and SNMPv2 support only trivial authentication based on plaintext community strings and are fundamentally insecure. The default SNMP community string that SNMPv1 and SNMPv2 agents commonly use is the word "public" with assigned "read" or "read and write" privileges; using this string leaves devices vulnerable to attack. If an unauthorized user were to gain access and had read/write privileges, that user could write data to the AP, compromising its original configuration. Organizations using SNMPv1 or SNMPv2 should change the community string as often as needed, taking into consideration that the string is transmitted in plaintext. For all versions of SNMP, privileges should be set to the least required (e.g., "read only").

■ **Using HTTP.** Most APs include an HTTP interface that provides administrators with a remotely accessible interface to manage device configuration. Normally, the only access control mechanism securing this interface is a user ID and password. Any user with those credentials can reconfigure the device to provide no security or change the encryption key so that no authorized users can associate with the AP. Because HTTP does not natively provide confidentiality security, it should be protected with SSL (i.e., HTTPS) or another encryption method. Also, administrators should consider enabling the HTTP interface only when it is needed (e.g., initial AP configuration) and keeping it disabled at all other times.

■ **Enabling logging.** Most APs have the ability to log security events. Enabling this on APs helps to ensure user accountability and also provides records that can be reviewed if malicious activity has occurred to better understand the nature of that activity.

6.3.3.2 WLAN configuration

■ **Changing default channel and power output.** The default channel and power output of APs should be configured appropriately. If APs are located near each other but are on different WLANs, a DoS can result from radio interference between the APs if they are operating on the same or conflicting channels. Organizations that incur radio interference should determine whether one or more nearby APs are using the same channel or a channel within five channels of their own and then choose a different channel. For example, channels 1, 6, and 11 can be used simultaneously by APs that are

---

[25] Any other management protocols on an AP that are not needed should also be disabled.

[26] See http://www.ietf.org/internet-drafts/draft-ietf-snmpv3-rfc2570bis-03.txt for additional information on why using SNMPv3 instead of SNMPv1 or SNMPv2 is strongly recommended.

close to each other without mutual interference. Organizations should perform a site survey to discover any sources of radio interference. The site survey should result in a report that proposes AP locations, determines coverage areas, and assigns radio channels to each AP. In addition, the power output of APs should be determined so that unneeded channel overlap can be minimized.

■ **Changing the SSID.** The SSID is an identifier that is sometimes referred to as the network name. Clients that wish to join a network scan an area for available networks and join by providing the correct SSID. The SSID, typically a null-terminated ASCII string, has a range from zero to 32 bytes (or characters). The default SSIDs used by many IEEE 802.11 WLAN vendors have been published and are well-known, so the default SSID values of APs should be changed from the factory default to an unidentifiable value or non-discrete name to help prevent users from accidentally connecting to the wrong WLAN and to make it somewhat more difficult for attackers to identify the organization's WLANs. Organizations should be aware that adversaries can capture the SSID by eavesdropping, so organizations should not rely on changing SSIDs to protect their WLANs.

■ **Avoiding pre-shared keys (PSK).** Organizations requiring robust authentication for WLANs should avoid the use of PSKs. In PSK environments, a secret passphrase is shared between STAs and APs. The PSK is generated by combining the WLAN's name and SSID with a passphrase, then hashing this multiple times. Keys derived from a passphrase shorter than approximately 20 characters provide relatively low levels of security and are subject to dictionary and rainbow attacks.[27] Changing the WLAN name or SSID will not improve the strength of the 256-bit PSK.

■ **Using MAC ACL functionality.** Many legacy IEEE 802.11 products have capabilities for restricting access to the WLAN based on MAC access control lists (ACL) that are distributed across APs. The MAC ACL grants or denies access to a WLAN client using a list of permissions designated by MAC address. However, the MAC ACL does not represent a strong defense mechanism by itself, because MAC addresses are transmitted in the clear from WLAN clients to APs, so they can be easily captured. A malicious user can spoof a MAC address by changing the actual MAC address on another computer to a MAC address that has access to the WLAN. MAC ACLs may be effective against casual eavesdropping but will not be effective against determined adversaries. Organizations should weigh the administrative burden of using MAC ACLs against the security they provide. In a medium-to-large network, the burden of establishing and maintaining MAC ACLs often exceeds their value as a countermeasure. In addition, most products support a limited number of MAC addresses in the MAC ACL, which may be insufficient for medium-to-large networks.

■ **Using DHCP.** The Dynamic Host Control Protocol (DHCP) can automatically assign IP addresses to devices that associate with an AP. The server assigns each device a dynamic IP address as long as the device's encryption settings are compatible with the WLAN. Because a DHCP server does not necessarily know which devices should have access to the WLAN, the server automatically assigns each device a valid IP address, including unauthorized devices. This risk can be somewhat mitigated by disabling DHCP and using static IP addresses for the WLAN client devices, but this solution is similar in effectiveness to using MAC ACL functionality. It will deter casual attackers but not determined adversaries, who can spoof IP addresses. Also, using static IP addresses may only be possible for relatively small networks, given the administrative overhead involved with assigning static IP addresses and the possible shortage of addresses. Statically assigning IP addresses to clients would also negate some of the key advantages of wireless networks, such as roaming.

■ **Maximizing the beacon interval.** The legacy IEEE 802.11 standard specifies the use of "beacon frames" to announce the existence of a wireless network. These beacons are transmitted from APs at regular intervals and allow a client station to identify and match configuration parameters to join a

---

[27] IEEE Std 802.11-2007, Part 11: Wireless LAN Medium Access Control (MAC) and Physical Layer (PHY) Specifications, p. 1128.

WLAN. APs can be configured to change the beacon interval, with a maximum value of approximately 67 seconds. Lengthening the beacon interval may make it slightly more difficult to passively locate a WLAN because the AP is not transmitting as frequently, and an adversary might have to perform active scanning using Probe Request messages to locate APs. However, lengthening the beacon interval can also make it more difficult or time-consuming for legitimate WLAN clients to find the WLAN. At best, lengthening the beacon interval is a mild deterrent for casual attackers; at worst, it is a significant disruption to operations.

6.3.4 Wireless Client Device Security

Devices that have been granted access to a legacy IEEE 802.11 WLAN should be properly secured to enhance the WLAN's security posture. Securing the infrastructure without properly securing the client devices renders the entire WLAN insecure. Client device security considerations include the following:

- **Automatic connection.** Client devices should be configured so that they do not automatically connect to WLANs. Permitting such automatic connections increases the risk of attack from malicious WLANs.

- **Personal firewalls.** Resources on WLANs have a higher risk of attack because they generally do not have the same degree of protection as internal resources. Personal firewalls increase device security by offering some protection against unwanted network connections initiated by other hosts.[28] Personal firewalls are software-based solutions that reside on a client device and are either client-managed or centrally-managed. Centrally-managed solutions provide a greater degree of protection because IT departments configure and remotely manage these solutions as opposed to leaving the management to the end user. Centrally-managed solutions allow organizations to modify client firewalls to protect against known vulnerabilities and to maintain a consistent security policy for all remote users. Some personal firewalls also have VPN capabilities.

- **Host-based intrusion detection and prevention systems (IDPS).** A host-based IDPS provides complementary security services to personal firewalls. Host-based IDPS software monitors and analyzes the internal state of a client device. Some products review logs to ensure that the system and applications are not functioning unexpectedly, such as applications inexplicably accessing or altering other portions of the system. Some host-based IDPS software products also monitor network communications and report or possibly block suspicious activity.

- **Antivirus.** Antivirus software can assist in preventing the spread of viruses, worms, and other malware between networked devices. Client devices that are at risk from known malware threats should have antivirus software installed and consistently updated to ensure that the newest updates and signatures are loaded on the client device. Organizations should ensure that antivirus software installed on client devices is properly configured to automatically receive updates.

- **Ad hoc mode.** If a client has IEEE 802.11 ad hoc mode enabled, other users may be able to inadvertently or maliciously connect to the client device, so the mode should be disabled if unneeded and feasible. Some clients do not provide a way to disable ad hoc mode.

- **IEEE 802.11 radio management.** Management of IEEE 802.11 radios is a simple way to improve security. Clients that have no business need for legacy IEEE 802.11 should have their wireless radios disabled by default. If feasible, users should disable the radio when not in use. A major risk is a client automatically connecting to an insecure or malicious WLAN without the user's knowledge; this risk can be mitigated by configuring clients so that they do not automatically connect to any WLAN

---

[28] See case study on the use of firewalls on laptops for telecommuters at
http://www.techrepublic.com/article.jhtml?id=r00520010328law01.htm.

they detect. In addition, client devices should be configured not to allow the simultaneous use of more than one network interface.

■ **Policy enforcement.** Client devices should be configured to comply with implemented WLAN policies. Policy enforcement and compliance for client devices takes several forms. Devices can be configured according to policy, such as disabling services or altering default configurations. In addition, policy-driven software solutions can be implemented on client devices to prevent or allow certain actions only when specific parameters are met. This type of software assists in ensuring that client devices and users comply with defined policies. For example, policy-based software can prevent client devices from having more than one network interface enabled at a time.

In addition to these considerations for client device security, organizations should also ensure that client devices are logically separated from the organization's wired networks. This is most commonly done by installing a firewall between the WLAN and the wired networks to enforce a security policy on the information flows. For example, such a firewall might permit the client devices to access only certain hosts or subnets on the wired networks using only particular protocols.

6.3.5 Patches, Upgrades, and Updates

Legacy IEEE 802.11 product vendors correct known software and hardware security vulnerabilities through patches, upgrades, or firmware updates. Network administrators should regularly check with vendors to identify new patches, upgrades, or updates and then apply them as needed, following the organization's procedures and processes.[29] In addition, many vendors have "security alert" email lists to advise customers of new vulnerabilities and attacks. Administrators can also check the National Vulnerability Database (NVD)[30] for a listing of all publicly known vulnerabilities in particular software or hardware.

6.3.6 Authentication

In general, effective authentication solutions are a reliable way to permit only authorized users to access a network. Authentication solutions include the use of usernames and passwords, smart cards, biometrics, PKI, or a combination of solutions (e.g., smart cards with PKI).[31] Authentication mechanisms can be integrated into a WLAN solution to enhance the security of the system. For example, if a VPN is being used to provide confidentiality and integrity protection for WLAN communications, the VPN could be configured to require user authentication.

---

[29] For more information, see NIST SP 800-40 Version 2, *Creating a Patch and Vulnerability Management Program*, http://csrc.nist.gov/publications/nistpubs/800-40-Ver2/SP800-40v2.pdf.

[30] NVD is located at http://nvd.nist.gov/.

[31] See FIPS PUB 196, *Entity Authentication Using Public Key Cryptography* at http://csrc.nist.gov/publications/fips/fips196/fips196.pdf.

Appendix A—Summary of IEEE 802.11 Standards

Table A-1 summarizes the various IEEE 802.11 standards. The table contains a description, purpose keywords and remarks, and estimated product availability for each standard.

Table A-1. Summary of IEEE 802.11 Standards

IEEE Standard	Description	Purpose Keywords and Other Remarks	Availability
802.11a	A physical layer standard that operates in the 5 GHz UNII radio band. It specifies eight available radio channels. (In some countries, 12 channels are permitted.) The maximum link rate is 54 Mbps per channel; maximum actual user data throughput is approximately half of that, and the throughput is shared by all users of the same radio channel. The data rate decreases as the distance between the user and the AP increases.	**Higher performance** In most office environments, the data throughput will be greater than for IEEE 802.11b. In addition, the greater number of non-overlapping radio channels (eight as opposed to three) provides better protection against possible interference from neighboring APs.	This standard was completed in 1999. Products are available now.
802.11b	This is a physical layer standard in the 2.4 GHz ISM radio band. Maximum link rate is 11 Mbps per channel, but maximum user throughput will be approximately half of this because the throughput is shared by all users of the same radio channel. The data rate decreases as the distance between the user and the AP increases.	**Performance** Installations may suffer from speed restrictions in the future, as the number of active users increase, and the limit of three non-overlapping channels may cause interference from neighboring APs.	This standard was completed in 1999. A wide variety of products has been available since 2001.
802.11d	This standard is supplementary to the MAC layer in IEEE 802.11 to promote worldwide use of IEEE 802.11 WLAN. It will allow APs to communicate information on the permissible radio channels with acceptable power levels for user devices. The IEEE 802.11 standards cannot legally operate in some countries; the purpose of 802.11d is to add features and restrictions to allow WLANs to operate within the rules of these countries.	**Promote worldwide use** In countries where the physical layer radio requirements are different from those in North America, the use of WLANs is lagging behind. Equipment manufacturers do not want to produce a wide variety of country-specific products, and users that travel do not want a bag full of country-specific WLAN PC cards. The outcome will be country-specific firmware solutions.	This standard was completed in 2001. Products are available now.
802.11e	This standard is supplementary to the MAC layer to provide QoS support for WLAN applications. It will apply to IEEE 802.11 physical standards a, b, and g. The purpose is to provide classes of service with managed levels of QoS for data, voice, and video applications.	**Quality of service** This standard provides some useful features for differentiating data traffic streams. It is essential for future audio and video distribution.	This standard was completed in 2005. Products are available now.

IEEE Standard	Description	Purpose Keywords and Other Remarks	Availability
802.11f	This is a "recommended practice" document that aims to achieve AP interoperability within a multi-vendor WLAN. The standard defines the registration of APs within a network and the interchange of information between APs when a user is handed over from one AP to another.	**Interoperability** This standard will work to increase vendor interoperability, reduce vendor lock-in, and allow multi-vendor infrastructures.	This recommended practice was completed in 2003. Products are available now.
802.11g	This is a physical layer standard for WLANs in the 2.4 GHz ISM radio band. The maximum link rate is 54 Mbps per channel whereas IEEE 802.11b offers 11 Mbps. The IEEE 802.11g standard uses orthogonal frequency-division multiplexing (OFDM) modulation but, for backward compatibility with IEEE 802.11b, it also supports complementary code-keying (CCK) modulation and, as an option for faster link rates, allows packet binary convolutional coding (PBCC) modulation.	**Higher performance with IEEE 802.11b backward compatibility** This standard provides speeds similar to IEEE 802.11a and backward compatibility with IEEE 802.11b.	This standard was completed in 2003. Products are available now.
802.11h	This standard is supplementary to the MAC layer to comply with European regulations for 5 GHz WLANs. European radio regulations for the 5 GHz band require products to have transmission power control (TPC) and dynamic frequency selection (DFS). TPC limits the transmitted power to the minimum needed to reach the farthest user. DFS selects the radio channel at the access point to minimize interference with other systems, particularly radar.	**European regulation compliance** This is necessary for products to operate in Europe. Completion of IEEE 802.11h provides better acceptability within Europe for IEEE-compliant 5 GHz WLAN products. A group that is rapidly dwindling will continue to support the alternative HyperLAN standard defined by the European Telecommunications Standard Institute (ETSI).	This standard was completed in 2003. Products are available now.
802.11i	This standard is supplementary to the MAC layer to improve security. It applies to IEEE 802.11 physical standards a, b, and g. It provides improved security over Wired Equivalent Privacy (WEP) with new encryption methods and authentication procedures. IEEE 802.1X forms a key part of IEEE 802.11i.	**Improved security** The IEEE 802.11i amendment defines two data confidentiality and integrity protocols for Robust Security Network Associations (RSNA): TKIP and Counter Mode with Cipher Block Chaining Message Authentication Code Protocol (CCMP), using AES. Federal agencies are required to use FIPS-validated cryptographic modules.[32] NIST SP 800-97 contains specific recommendations and guidance for IEEE 802.11i.	This standard was completed in 2004. Products are available now.

---

[32] Information about NIST's Cryptographic Module Validation program can be found at http://csrc.nist.gov/groups/STM/index.html. FIPS PUB 140-2 (http://csrc.nist.gov/publications/fips/fips140-2/fips1402.pdf) describes the generic security requirements; the implementation guide includes specific implementation guidance for IEEE 802.11. Lists of FIPS-approved cryptographic products can be found at http://csrc.nist.gov/groups/STM/cmvp/.

IEEE Standard	Description	Purpose Keywords and Other Remarks	Availability
802.11k	This standard defines Radio Resource Measurement enhancements to provide management and maintenance interfaces to higher layers for mobile WLANs.	**Resource radio management** This standard will enable seamless Basic Service Set (BSS) transitions between WLANs through the discovery of the best available AP and improve network traffic by distributing users to under-used APs.	Draft 11 was approved in January 2008. Final ratification has not yet occurred.
802.11m	This is a supplementary maintenance standard to the IEEE 802.11-1999 (reaff. 2003) standard.	**Editorial maintenance** This initiative is to perform editorial maintenance, corrections, improvements, clarifications, and interpretations to the IEEE 802.11-1999 (reaff. 2003) Wireless LAN Medium Access Control (MAC) and Physical Layer (PHY) specifications standard.	This standard was completed and is part of 802.11-2007.
802.11n	This standard investigated the possibility of improving the IEEE 802.11 standard to provide high throughput at a theoretical 300 Mbps.	**Increased data throughput** The purpose of this standard is to improve the IEEE 802.11 WLAN user experience by providing significantly higher throughput using MIMO antennas and receivers and different coding schemes.	This standard is expected to be completed in 2009.
802.11p	This standard is an amendment of IEEE 802.11 to support communication between vehicles and the roadside and between vehicles while operating at speeds up to a minimum of 200 kilometers/hour for communication ranges up to 1,000 meters. The amendment will support communications in the 5 GHz bands—specifically 5.850–5.925 GHz band within North America—with the aim to enhance the mobility and safety of all forms of surface transportation, including rail and marine. Amendments to the Physical (PHY) and MAC layers will be limited to those required to support communications under these operating environments within the 5 GHz bands. This standard is also referred to as the Wireless Access for Vehicular Environment (WAVE).	**Wireless access for vehicles** This standard amends the existing IEEE 802.11 standard to make it suitable for interoperable communications to and between vehicles. The primary reasons for this amendment include the unique transport environments and the very short latencies required (some applications must complete multiple data exchanges within 4 to 50 milliseconds).	This standard is scheduled to be completed in April 2009.
802.11r	This standard is supplementary to the IEEE 802.11 Medium Access Control (MAC) layer standards and creates improvements to minimize or eliminate the amount of time data connectivity between the Station (STA) and the Distribution System (DS) during a BSS transition.	**Fast BSS transitions** This standard improves BSS handoffs within IEEE 802.11 networks. This is a critical component to support real-time constraints imposed by applications such as Voice over Internet Protocol (VoIP).	This standard is scheduled to be published in mid-2008.

IEEE Standard	Description	Purpose Keywords and Other Remarks	Availability
802.11s	This standard defined the IEEE 802.11 ESS Mesh with an IEEE 802.11 Wireless Distribution System (WDS) using the IEEE 802.11 MAC/PHY layers that supports both broadcast/multicast and unicast delivery over self-configuring multi-hop topologies.	**ESS mesh networking** This standard provides a protocol for auto-configuring paths between APs over self-configuring multi-hop topologies in a WDS to support both broadcast/multicast and unicast traffic in an ESS Mesh using the four-address frame format or an extension.	This standard is scheduled to be completed in 2008.
802.11t	This is a "recommended practice" and will provide a set of performance metrics, measurement methodologies, and test conditions to enable measuring and predicting the performance of IEEE 802.11 WLAN devices and networks at the component and application level as a recommended practice.	**Wireless performance protection** This standard enables testing, comparison, and deployment planning of IEEE 802.11 WLAN products so that performance and products specifications can be captured through common and accepted set of performance metrics, measurement methodologies and test conditions.	This recommended practice is scheduled to be completed in 2008.
802.11u	This standard is an amendment to the IEEE 802.11 MAC and PHY layers to support InterWorking with External Networks.	**Internetworking with external networks** This will provide amendments to the IEEE 802.11 PHY/MAC layers, which will enable InterWorking with other networks and granting of limited access, based on a relationship with an external network. This includes both enhanced protocol exchanges across the air interface and provision of primitives to support required interactions with higher layers for InterWorking.	This standard is in the proposal evaluation stages and a scheduled completion date has not been set.
802.11v	This standard will create amendments to provide Wireless Network Management enhancements to the IEEE 802.11 MAC, and PHY layers to allow configuration of client devices connected to the network.	**Wireless network management** This will provide amendments to the IEEE 802.11 PHY/MAC layers that enable management of attached stations in a centralized or in a distributed fashion (e.g., monitoring, configuring, and updating) through a layer 2 mechanism. Although the IEEE 802.11k Task Group is defining messages to retrieve information from the station, the ability to configure the station is not within its scope. The proposed Task Group will also create an Access Port Management Information Base (AP MIB).	This standard is in the early proposal stages and a scheduled completion date has not been set.

IEEE Standard	Description	Purpose Keywords and Other Remarks	Availability
802.11w	This standard will enhance IEEE 802.11 MAC layer security for selected management frames by providing data integrity, data origin authenticity, replay protection, data confidentiality, and other security features.	**Management frame protection** This will extend the use of IEEE 802.11i to selected management frames to increase the overall security of IEEE 802.11-based networks. The increased level of security is intended to mitigate malicious network-based attacks, such as DoS attacks. In addition, this amendment will provide security for sensitive network information that will be included in transmissions outlined in several new amendments, including IEEE 802.11r, IEEE 802.11k, and IEEE 802.11y.	The standard is under development and is expected to be completed and ratified in 2008.

Appendix B—Glossary of Terms

Selected terms used in the publication are defined below.

Access Point (AP): A device that logically connects wireless client devices operating in infrastructure to one another and provides access to a distribution system, if connected, which is typically an organization's enterprise wired network.

Ad Hoc Network: A wireless network that dynamically connects wireless client devices to each other without the use of an infrastructure device, such as an access point or a base station.

Flooding: An attack in which an attacker sends large numbers of wireless messages at a high rate to prevent the wireless network from processing legitimate traffic.

Infrastructure Network: A wireless network that requires the use of an infrastructure device, such as an access point or a base station, to facilitate communication between client devices.

Jamming: An attack in which a device is used to emit electromagnetic energy on a wireless network's frequency to make it unusable.

Media Access Control (MAC): A unique 48-bit value that is assigned to a particular wireless network interface by the manufacturer.

Range: The maximum possible distance for communicating with a wireless network infrastructure or wireless client.

Robust Security Network (RSN): A wireless security network that only allows the creation of Robust Security Network Associations (RSNA).

Robust Security Network Association (RSNA): A logical connection between communicating IEEE 802.11 entities established through the IEEE 802.11i key management scheme, also known as the four-way handshake.

Service Set Identifier (SSID): A name assigned to a WLAN that allows stations to distinguish one WLAN from another.

Station (STA): A client device in a wireless network.

Wired Equivalent Privacy (WEP): A security protocol, specified in the IEEE 802.11 standard, that is designed to provide a WLAN with a level of security and privacy comparable to what is usually expected of a wired LAN. WEP is no longer considered a viable encryption mechanism due to known weaknesses.

Wireless Bridge: A device that links two wired networks, generally operating at two different physical locations, through wireless communications.

Wireless Local Area Network (WLAN): A group of wireless APs and associated infrastructure within a limited geographic area, such as an office building or building campus, that is capable of radio communications. WLANs are usually implemented as extensions of existing wired LANs to provide enhanced user mobility.

Appendix C—Acronyms and Abbreviations

Selected acronyms and abbreviations used in the publication are defined below.

ACL	Access Control List
AES	Advanced Encryption Standard
ANSI	American National Standards Institute
AP	Access Point
BSS	Basic Service Set
CCK	Complementary Code-Keying
CCMP	Cipher Block Chaining Message Authentication Code Protocol
CRC	Cyclic Redundancy Check
CTIA	Cellular Telecommunications and Internet Association
DFS	Dynamic Frequency Selection
DHCP	Dynamic Host Control Protocol
DISA	Defense Information Systems Agency
DoD	Department of Defense
DoS	Denial of Service
DS	Distribution System
EAP	Extensible Authentication Protocol
ESS	Extended Service Set
ETSI	European Telecommunications Standard Institute
FIPS	Federal Information Processing Standard
FISMA	Federal Information Systems Management Act
GHz	Gigahertz
HMAC	Hash Message Authentication Code
HTTP	HyperText Transfer Protocol
IBSS	Interdependent Basic Service Set
ICV	Integrity Check Value
IDPS	Intrusion Detection Prevention System
IEEE	Institute of Electrical and Electronics Engineers
IP	Internet Protocol
IPsec	Internet Protocol Security
IPX	Internet Packet Exchange
ISM	Industrial, Scientific, and Medical
IT	Information Technology
ITL	Information Technology Laboratory
IV	Initialization Vector
LAN	Local Area Network
MAC	Medium Access Control

Mbps	Megabits per second
MHz	Megahertz
MIB	Management Information Base
MIC	Message Integrity Check
MIMO	Multiple Input, Multiple Output
NIC	Network Interface Card
NIST	National Institute of Standards and Technology
NVD	National Vulnerability Database
OFDM	Orthogonal Frequency Division Multiplexing
OMB	Office of Management and Budget
PBCC	Packet Binary Convolutional Coding
PC	Personal Computer
PDA	Personal Digital Assistant
PHY	Physical Layer
PIN	Personal Identification Number
PIV	Personal Identity Verification
PKI	Public Key Infrastructure
PMK	Pairwise Master Key
PSK	Pre-Shared Key
PUB	Publication
QoS	Quality of Service
RF	Radio Frequency
RFID	Radio Frequency Identification
RSA	Rivest-Shamir-Adelman
RSN	Robust Security Network
RSNA	Robust Security Network Association
SHS	Secure Hash Standard
SNMP	Simple Network Management Protocol
SP	Special Publication
SSID	Service Set Identifier
SSL	Secure Sockets Layer
STA	Station
TCP	Transmission Control Protocol
TKIP	Temporal Key Integrity Protocol
TLS	Transport Layer Security
TPC	Transmission Power Control
UNII	Unlicensed National Information Infrastructure
VLAN	Virtual Local Area Network
VPN	Virtual Private Network
VoIP	Voice over Internet Protocol
WAVE	Wireless Access for Vehicular Environment

WDS	Wireless Distribution System
WEP	Wired Equivalent Privacy
WIDPS	Wireless Intrusion Detection and Prevention System
WLAN	Wireless Local Area Network
WPA	Wi-Fi Protected Access
WPA2	Wi-Fi Protected Access 2
XOR	Exclusive OR

Appendix D—References

The list below provides references for the publication.

Anderson, Gustave et al., "A Secure Wireless Agent-based Testbed," *Proceedings of the Second IEEE International Information Assurance Workshop*, 2004.

Baghaei, Nilufar and Hunt, Ray, "IEEE 802.11 Wireless LAN Security Performance Using Multiple Clients," *Proceedings of the 12th IEEE International Conference on Networks*, 2004.

Bargh, Mortaza et al., "Fast Authentication Methods for Handovers Between IEEE 802.11 Wireless LANs," *Proceedings of the 2nd ACM International Workshop on Wireless Mobile Applications and Services on WLAN Hotspots*, 2004.

Becker, Bernd, Eisinger, Jochen, and Winterer, Peter, "Securing Wireless Networks in a University Environment," *Proceedings of the Third IEEE International Conference on Pervasive Computing and Communications Workshops*, 2005.

Carli, Marco, Neri, A., and Rossetti, A., "Integrated Security Architecture for WLAN," *Proceedings of the IEEE 10th International Conference on Telecommunications*, 2003.

Chen, Jyh-Cheng, Jiang, Ming-Chia, and Liu, Yi-Wen, "Wireless LAN Security and IEEE 802.11i," *IEEE Wireless Communications*, February 2005.

Chen, Jyh-Cheng, Liu, Yi-Wen, and Wang, Yu-Ping, "Design and Implementation of WIRE1x." *Proceedings of Taiwan Area Network Conference*, 2003.

Edney, Jon and Arbaugh, William A., *Real 802.11 Security: Wi-Fi Protected Access and 802.11i*, Addison-Wesley, 2004.

Fluhrer, Scott, Mantin, Itsik, and Shamir, Adi, "Weaknesses in the Key Schedule Algorithm of RC4," *Proceedings of the 4th Annual Workshop on Selected Areas of Cryptography*, 2001.

Gast, Matthew S., *802.11® Wireless Networks: The Definitive Guide (2nd Edition)*, O'Reilly Media, 2005.

He, Changhua, and Mitchell, John, "Analysis of the 802.11i 4-Way Handshake," *Proceedings of the 2004 ACM Workshop on Wireless Security*, 2004.

IEEE Standard 802.11, 1999 Edition.

IEEE Standard 802.11i, 2004 Edition. Also available at
http://standards.ieee.org/getieee802/download/802.11i-2004.pdf.

IEEE Standard 802.1X, 2004 Edition. Also available at
http://standards.ieee.org/getieee802/download/802.1X-2004.pdf.

IEEE Standard 802.11, 2007 Edition. Also available at
http://standards.ieee.org/getieee802/download/802.11-2007.pdf

Matsunaga, Yasuhiko et al., "Secure Authentication System for Public WLAN Roaming," *Proceedings of the First ACM International Workshop on Wireless Mobile Applications and Services on WLAN Hotspots*, 2003.

Mitsuyama, Yukio et al., "Embedded Architecture of IEEE 802.11i Cipher Algorithms," *Proceedings of the IEEE International Symposium on Consumer Electronics*, 2004.

O'Hara, Bob and Petrick, Al, *IEEE 802.11 Handbook: A Designer's Companion*, IEEE Press, 2001.

Schmoyer, Tim, Lim, Yu-Xi, and Owen, Henry, "Wireless Intrusion Detection and Response: A Case Study Using the Classic Man-in-the-Middle Attack," *Proceedings of IEEE Wireless Communication and Networking Conference 2004*, 2004.

Smyth, Neil, McLoone, Máire, and McCanny, John, "Reconfigurable Hardware Acceleration of WLAN Security," *IEEE Workshop on Signal Processing Systems (SiPS) Design & Implementation*, 2004.

Šorman, Matija, Kovač, Tomislav, and Maurović, Damir, "Implementing Improved WLAN Security," *46th International Symposium Electronics in Marine*, 2004.

Wool, Avishai, "A Note on the Fragility of the 'Michael' Message Integrity Code," *IEEE Transactions on Wireless Communications*, Vol. 3 No. 5, September 2004.

You, Liyu and Jamshaid, Kamran, "Novel Applications for 802.11x Enabled Wireless Networked Home," *2004 IEEE Consumer Communications and Networking Conference*, 2004.

Appendix E—Online Resources

The lists below provide examples of online resources related to wireless network security that may be helpful to readers.

Documents

Name	URL
Deploying WPA™ and WPA2™ in the Enterprise	http://www.wi-fi.org/white_papers/whitepaper-022705-deployingwpawpa2enterprise/
The DoD Public Key Infrastructure and Public Key-Enabling Frequently Asked Questions	http://iase.disa.mil/pki/faq-pki-pke-may-2004.doc
Extensible Authentication Protocol (EAP) Registry	http://www.iana.org/assignments/eap-numbers
FIPS 140-2, Security Requirements for Cryptographic Modules	http://csrc.nist.gov/publications/fips/fips140-2/fips1402.pdf
FIPS 180-2, Secure Hash Standard (SHS)	http://csrc.nist.gov/publications/fips/fips180-2/fips180-2withchangenotice.pdf
FIPS 197, Advanced Encryption Standard (AES)	http://csrc.nist.gov/publications/fips/fips197/fips-197.pdf
FIPS 199, Standards for Security Categorization of Federal Information and Information Systems	http://csrc.nist.gov/publications/fips/fips199/FIPS-PUB-199-final.pdf
GAO-05-383, Information Security: Federal Agencies Need to Improve Controls over Wireless Networks	http://www.gao.gov/new.items/d05383.pdf
GRS 24, Information Technology Operations and Management Records	http://www.archives.gov/records-mgmt/ardor/grs24.html
Michael: An Improved MIC for 802.11 WEP	http://grouper.ieee.org/groups/802/11/Documents/DocumentHolder/2-020.zip
NIST Personal Identity Verification (PIV) Project	http://csrc.nist.gov/groups/SNS/piv/index.html
NIST SP 800-30, Risk Management Guide for Information Technology Systems	http://csrc.nist.gov/publications/nistpubs/800-30/sp800-30.pdf
NIST SP 800-32, Introduction to Public Key Technology and the Federal PKI Infrastructure	http://csrc.nist.gov/publications/nistpubs/800-32/sp800-32.pdf
NIST SP 800-40 Version 2.0, Creating a Patch and Vulnerability Management Program	http://csrc.nist.gov/publications/nistpubs/800-40-Ver2/SP800-40v2.pdf
NIST SP 800-41, Guidelines on Firewalls and Firewall Policy	http://csrc.nist.gov/publications/nistpubs/800-41/sp800-41.pdf
NIST SP 800-41 Revision 1 (Draft), Guidelines on Firewalls and Firewall Policy	http://csrc.nist.gov/publications/PubsDrafts.html
NIST SP 800-50, Building an Information Technology Security Awareness and Training Program	http://csrc.nist.gov/publications/nistpubs/800-50/NIST-SP800-50.pdf
NIST SP 800-52, Guidelines for the Selection and Use of Transport Layer Security (TLS) Implementations	http://csrc.nist.gov/publications/nistpubs/800-52/SP800-52.pdf
NIST SP 800-53 Revision 2, Recommended Security Controls for Federal Information Systems	http://csrc.nist.gov/publications/nistpubs/800-53-Rev2/sp800-53-rev2-final.pdf
NIST SP 800-63 Version 1.0.2, Electronic Authentication Guideline	http://csrc.nist.gov/publications/nistpubs/800-63/SP800-63V1_0_2.pdf

Name	URL
NIST SP 800-63-1 (Draft), *Electronic Authentication Guideline*	http://csrc.nist.gov/publications/PubsDrafts.html
NIST SP 800-64, *Security Considerations in the Information System Development Life Cycle*	http://csrc.nist.gov/publications/nistpubs/800-64/NIST-SP800-64.pdf
NIST SP 800-70, *Security Configuration Checklists Program for IT Products—Guidance for Checklists Users and Developers*	http://checklists.nist.gov/docs/SP_800-70_20050526.pdf
NIST SP 800-77, *Guide to IPsec VPNs*	http://csrc.nist.gov/publications/nistpubs/800-77/sp800-77.pdf
NIST SP 800-94, *Guide to Intrusion Detection and Prevention Systems (IDPS)*	http://csrc.nist.gov/publications/nistpubs/800-94/SP800-94.pdf
NIST SP 800-97, *Establishing Wireless Robust Security Networks: A Guide to IEEE 802.11i*	http://csrc.nist.gov/publications/nistpubs/800-97/SP800-97.pdf
NIST SP 800-98, *Guidelines for Securing Radio Frequency Identification (RFID) Systems*	http://csrc.nist.gov/publications/nistpubs/800-98/SP800-98_RFID-2007.pdf
NIST SP 800-100, *Information Security Handbook: A Guide for Managers*	http://csrc.nist.gov/publications/nistpubs/800-100/SP800-100-Mar07-2007.pdf
NIST SP 800-111, *Guide to Storage Encryption Technologies for End User Devices*	http://csrc.nist.gov/publications/nistpubs/800-111/SP800-111.pdf
NIST SP 800-114, *User's Guide to Securing External Devices for Telework and Remote Access*	http://csrc.nist.gov/publications/nistpubs/800-114/SP800-114.pdf
NIST SP 800-121 (Draft), *Guide to Bluetooth Security*	http://csrc.nist.gov/publications/PubsDrafts.html
NIST SP 800-124 (Draft), *Guidelines on Cell Phone and PDA Security*	http://csrc.nist.gov/publications/PubsDrafts.html

Resource Sites

Name	URL
Cellular Telecommunications and Internet Association (CTIA) The Wireless Association	http://www.ctia.org/
Federal Communications Commission	http://www.fcc.gov/
FIPS-validated Cryptographic Modules	http://csrc.nist.gov/groups/STM/cmvp/index.html
IEEE 802.11 Working Group on Wireless Local Area Networks	http://www.ieee802.org/11/
International Engineering Consortium, EAP Methods for 802.11 Wireless LAN Security	http://www.iec.org/online/tutorials/eap_methods/
NIST National Checklist Program	http://checklists.nist.gov/
NIST National Vulnerability Database (NVD)	http://nvd.nist.gov/
SNMPv3 Specifications and Documentation	http://www.snmp.com/snmpv3/
Wi-Fi Alliance	http://www.wi-fi.org/
Wi-Fi Alliance Certified Products	http://certifications.wi-fi.org/wbcs_certified_products.php?lang=en
Wireless Vulnerabilities & Exploits Homepage	http://www.wirelessve.org/

www.ingramcontent.com/pod-product-compliance
Lightning Source LLC
Chambersburg PA
CBHW060506060326
40689CB00020B/4647